TROPICAL

BAR BOOK

CHARLES SCHUMANN

TROPICAL
BAR BOOK

DRINKS & STORIES

Illustrated and designed
by Günter Mattei

Compiled by
Jürgen Woldt

STEWART, TABORI & CHANG
NEW YORK

One of sour,
two of sweet,
three of strong,
and four of weak.

**The proportions of lemon,
sugar, rum, and water,
from an old drink recipe.**

The goddess made for me a cup of tea,
with a spot of rum;
But she herself drank only the rum,
without a spot of tea.

Heinrich Heine

Originally published as Schumann's Tropical Barbuch
Copyright © 1986 by Wilhelm Heyne Verlag
GmbH & Co. KG, München
Translation copyright © 1989 by Stewart, Tabori & Chang, Inc.
Acknowledgments and credits appear on page 158
and constitute an extension of this page.

Cover and adaptation of design for this edition
by Jeff Batzli

Published in 1989 by
Stewart, Tabori & Chang, Inc.
740 Broadway, New York, New York 10003

Distributed in the U.S. by Workman Publishing
708 Broadway, New York, New York 10003
Distributed in Canada by Canadian Manda Group
P.O. Box 920 Station U, Toronto, Ontario M8Z 5P9
Distributed in all other territories by
Little, Brown and Company, International Division
34 Beacon Street, Boston, Massachusetts 02108

Library of Congress Cataloging-in-Publication Data

Schumann, Charles.
[Schumann's Tropical Barbuch. English]
Tropical bar book : drinks & stories / Charles Schumann ;
illustrated and designed by Günter Mattei ; compiled by
Jürgen Woldt ; [text translated from the German by Russell
Stockman].
p.   cm.
Translation of: Schumann's Tropical Barbuch.
Includes index.
ISBN 1-55670-065-2
1. Liquors.   2. Cocktails.   3. Beverages.   I. Woldt,
Jürgen
II. Title.
TX951. S42513   1989
641.2′1—dc19
89-4171
CIP

Printed in Japan.

10 9 8 7 6 5 4 3 2 1

Contents

CONTENTS

For some time now, no proper bar has been complete without its bottles of rum, tequila, and cachaça on the shelves. Any professional bartender will tell you that concoctions of tropical liquors, juices, and syrups have now become as popular as the traditional American cocktails.

Rum was probably the first distilled alcohol and in the history of mixed drinks it has experienced, like gin, repeated ups and downs. Rum's last real heyday was during the twenties in Cuba, where thirsty Americans descended in droves in their flight from Prohibition. Cuba's bartenders simply substituted rum for gin or whiskey in the classic mixed drinks until a few of the more imaginative came up with the rum-based drinks that have since become classics themselves.

The last few years have seen a decided trend away from straight hard liquors and toward tropical drinks. In fact, thanks to these more exotic offerings, bar patrons have again found a taste for mixed drinks of all kinds.

At first, the number of tropical drinks was relatively limited. Those with a sweet tooth ordered Planter's Punch or Piña Coladas, while the hard drinkers made do with a Mai Tai or a Zombie. Now, thanks to the greater availability of exotic juices and syrups, a whole rainbow of new and interesting cocktails has been created.

With all of these new ingredients, it might be tempting to simply toss them into one's shaker and see what happens; but nothing could be more fatal. Most fruit flavorings have such a distinct aroma that they mix well with only a limited number of others. It is important to make this clear; many highly touted tropical drink recipes strike me as altogether ludicrous. This book features roughly 150 drinks— to my mind the only ones that deserve to be included. Of these, my own creations are marked with an asterisk and a date. I have grouped similar drinks together— most, in this instance, being based on rum. Hot drinks and nonalcoholic ones are dealt with in separate sections. The final chapters cover tequila, mescal, and cachaça. To assist you in stocking and understanding your bar, I include chapters on tropical fruits, additives, and seasonings, on the history and production of rum, and on the basic qualities of the various groups of drinks.

And finally, you'll find a number of selections from well-known writers, all of them having to do with bar life and drinking in the tropics. Some on-the-spot reporting and stories by native Caribbean authors are also included. All together, these pieces conjure up the unique quality of tropical life, outside of bars as well as in them.

CHARLES SCHUMANN

He was drinking another of the frozen daiquiris with no sugar in it and as he lifted it, heavy and the glass frost-rimmed, he looked at the clear part below the frappéd top and it reminded him of the sea. The frappéd part of the drink was like the wake of a ship and the clear part was the way the water looked when the bow cut it when you were in shallow water over marl bottom. That was almost the exact color."

The color in question was turquoise. The man who wrote this famous description of a glass filled with lime juice, white rum, and crushed ice had seen a great deal of such water, above the white coral sand of Caribbean lagoons, along the reefs of the Bimini Islands, off the palm-lined shores of the Bahamas, and in the mangrove-circled bays of Cayo Cruz off the coast of Cuba. His favorite place to order the drink that reminded him of his voyages through the lagoons was Havana's La Floridita bar. And his favorite bartender at La Floridita was Constantino Ribailagua—Constante for short—the acknowledged king of Cuba's bartenders in the twenties and thirties, and creator of a number of tropical cocktails now considered classics. One of these Constante named after his frequent patron and daiquiri fancier, dubbing it the Hemingway Special.

Stories about rum and drinking in the tropics come in countless variations. Some tell of pirates, colonial intrigues, or sightings of phantom ships; others are simple bar yarns, commemorating outrageous drinking bouts in long-vanished dives. Many are the stuff of legend. Hemingway too became a legend as the inveterate barfly. When in Havana he would only drink daiquiris at La Floridita, and only as served by Constante. At the equally famous Bodeguita del Medio he would order Mojito Criollo, the most typically Cuban of cocktails. This was when it seemed that everyone was drinking fizzes and cobblers, collinses and daisies, if not at one of these bars, then at the Café Los Bancos, the Ambos Mundos, the Telégrafo, or the bar in the Sevilla Biltmore. Havana in the twenties and thirties witnessed an unprecedented bar boom, and suddenly rum became the focus of a new, international drinking craze. It was an American who dubbed this period "the golden age of the cocktail." Yet it was not simply the lure of the tropics that brought everyone to Havana—far from it. Cuba happened to fill a vacuum in the market, just as soon as Prohibition became the law in the United States in 1919. In no time at all, hordes of North American drinkers were breaking through "Rum Row," the twelve-mile dry zone off the nation's coastline, and heading for Cuba. In consequence, barkeeps and hoteliers from all over the world found their way to Cuba as well. Ultimately the new Havana bars became so popular that an American airline had to schedule a special rum flight between Florida and Cuba. Placards on the street corners in Miami urged parched Americans to "fly to Havana and bathe in Bacardi." Even Al Capone got into the act. To the west of Havana he built his own rum distillery, a link in his flourishing smuggling industry.

One thinks of this period of Prohibition as the time when rum became the staple of the tropical bar. But in fact it was an earlier generation of Americans who discovered the delight of rum in mixed drinks. The soldiers sent to Cuba to drive out the Spaniards at the end of the nineteenth century brought no liquor of their own with them. Instead, they had to make do with the native rum, which they promptly added to the one drink they did have with them, Coca-Cola. They named the combination after the familiar battle cry heard at the front: "Cuba Libre!"

That rum should have experienced a boom during these decades of war and unrest seems only logical, given the earlier history of this by-product of sugar production. Rum had played a role in the earliest wars of the colonial period—and for that matter in what was possibly the most vicious instance of genocide in mankind's history.

An entry in the logbook of Christopher Columbus—better known in Spanish as Cristóbal Colón—during his second visit to the West Indies in 1493, indicates the beginning of the slaughter. After meeting for the first time with the Caribbean Indians, noting that they "shared everything most cordially," and that to them "weapons were altogether unknown," Columbus took seven of that cheerful people captive. On presenting them to his king, he suggested that it would henceforth be a good idea to "keep all of the island natives . . . on their islands as slaves," for with "a mere fifty men one could subdue the entire populace and force them to do anything at all." It was on that same journey that Columbus brought the first sugarcane to the West Indies.

As it happened, the majority of the Indians were not so easily exploited after all. They did not welcome slavery, whether in the gold mines or on the new sugarcane plantations, and they resented their forced conversion to Christianity. The colonists therefore set about the annihilation of the native inhabitants on an unprecedented scale. The first to begin the slaughter were the Spanish and Portuguese, but in time they were joined by the French, the English, the Scandinavians, and the Germans. Of the latter, the most notorious was the patrician Welser family from Augsburg, whose policy of decapitating the Indians made it infamous throughout South America. The monk Bartolome de Las Casas was an eyewitness to the slaughter. In his chronicle, written between 1527 and 1566 but only published three centuries later, he tells us

that no fewer than thirty million Indians were destroyed during the first years of the conquest. Of the Caribbean Indians, a mere 2,500 survive today—on a reservation in the island nation of Dominica. Lichtenberg, a philosopher of the Enlightenment in eighteenth-century Göttingen, once made the observation that "the American who first discovered Columbus made a rotten discovery."

The first documentary mention of West Indian rum dates from the mid-seventeenth century. In a description of Barbados from 1651 we read, "The chief alcohol produced on this island is *rumbullion*, alias *kill devil*." It may be that the word "rum" does indeed derive from *rumbullion*, meaning riot or uprising, but it is equally likely that it comes from the Malay *brum*, designating the liquor made from sugar (it was in East Asia that sugarcane was first cultivated). Or it may simply be an abbreviation of the Latin term for sugar, *saccharum officinarum*.

The sugar trade was all-important to the colonial powers during the first century of their rule, and soon the presence of large and wealthy sugar plantations once again turned the Caribbean region into a battlefield. This time the Europeans made do with killing each other, rather than the native inhabitants. The conflict played out on all of the world's oceans in the early years of the eighteenth century, but especially in the Caribbean, is known to historians as the War of the Spanish Suc-

cession. It would be just as accurate to call it the first world war of history. Engaged in the struggle were not only the warships of the various states, but also whole fleets of pirate vessels, each furnished by one or another sovereign with letters of marque, royal authorization to plunder, kill, and conquer. Whatever the flag he served, every sailor could count on his daily ration of rum.

Neither piracy nor war could hamper the sugar trade. It continued to flourish along with the traffic in rum, that easily distilled by-product of the sugar refinery. In the eighteenth century, rum came to function as an international currency. It was a standard form of payment to sailors, to the North American Indians in the fur trade, and above all in the buying and selling of African slaves—the next dark chapter in the history of rum.

It is uncertain just how many Africans were transported to the New World after the majority of its native Indians had been exterminated. Estimates range from thirty to fifty million. We do know that in the United States the number of slaves originally introduced had multiplied eleven times by the time of abolition. In the islands of the West Indies, however, only a third of the original number remained. Why the discrepancy? Caribbean planters could never agree whether it was more profitable to spare their slaves, permitting them to marry and have children, or to quickly work them to death in the cane-

fields and rum factories and simply replace them with new ones. Most of them opted for the latter treatment. It was rare for a field slave to survive as long as five years on a Caribbean plantation; and of course one in five had already succumbed on the high seas.

The history of slavery is largely dependent on the late eighteenth-century white man's insatiable craving for sugar and rum. Demand for the sweetener and its soothing by-product was enormous, both in Europe and North America. Even by today's standards it seems astonishing. Per capita consumption of rum in North America was as high as eighteen liters a year—no small thanks to the unquenchable thirst of the Revolutionary soldier. Today, Americans consume a total of six liters of distilled spirits per capita a year.

Factories equipped to transform imported West Indian molasses into rum sprang up around New York and throughout New England. With these in place, the infamous "three-cornered trade" could proceed. This was the blood-drenched exchange that brought West Indian molasses to the distilleries of New England, New England rum to the slave traders of Africa, and African slaves to the sugar plantations of the West Indies. Such commerce in horror only ended with the abolition of slavery—in 1836 in the English colonies of the West Indies, 1848 in the French ones—once the discovery of less expensive beet sugar had broken the monopoly of the sugar barons.

Nearly all of the alcohol in the exotic drinks served to tourists throughout the tropics, whether on islands in the South Pacific or the Indian Ocean, in Brazil, Hawaii, or the Seychelles, is produced in the Caribbean. The world's infatuation with rum began here, and it was here that tropical drinks and cocktails were developed. To be sure, the history of rum is simultaneously the history of white colonizers and their victims, a sordid tale that continues into our own century. Yet none of this need deter one from lounging in the warm trade wind on some coral beach and sipping Planter's Punch while being lulled by the lapping of the waves of the lagoon and the whisper of palm fronds. Or from gazing, like Hemingway in La Floridita, into one's daiquiri glass in some northern bar and envisioning the light turquoise of the Caribbean Sea. To indulge in such reverie is to succumb to one of the northerner's more seductive myths, the myth of a tropical paradise. Tropical drinks are but a delightful accompaniment to the age-old dream. A Jamaican saying puts things in somewhat clearer perspective: "God caused men to raise themselves up onto their feet; rum sees to it that they fall over again."

Anyone can verify this easily for himself.

To the dedicated rum drinker, the location of the distillery and the method it employs are all-important. Connoisseurs distinguish as many different flavors as do wine experts. Yet all types of rum are derived from the same raw material: the sap of the sugarcane. Most often, they are made from molasses—the brown, viscous substance left behind as the sugar is boiled out. Sugarcane contains a pulp consisting of up to 90 percent sap, which is in turn made up of as much as 18 percent sugar.

The molasses by-product still contains a large amount of sugar that has not been crystallized out in the boiling process. So much, in fact, that it cannot begin to ferment until it is thinned with water. To the diluted molasses, skimming and dun-der are added before the fermentation that will yield rum. Skimming is the foam that collects on the surface when the sap is boiled; dunder is a nonalcoholic sediment left in the still after previous distillation, consisting of yeast, bacteria, and various acids. Both of these additives help determine the taste and aroma of the finished rum.

Some brands, notably the French ones from Martinique, are distilled directly from the pure sugar sap or syrup. It was long ago found to be more economical to make double use of the sap, first by boiling out the sugar and then making rum from what is left in the next-door distillery, but demand for cane sugar on the world's markets has now declined to the point that the traditional link between refinery and distillery has been weakened.

Each distiller preserves the secret of just which flavorings are introduced into the mash of molasses, water, skimming, and dunder. Typical additions are raisins, pineapple, cinnamon, and vanilla. Distillers are especially guarded about the type of yeast and the bacteria culture employed to trigger the process of fermentation. The process is relatively swift in the case of rum and can easily reach its peak in as little as twenty to thirty hours. However, many distillers prefer to prolong it for as much as twelve days, through careful manipulation of temperature, for slower fermentation produces a stronger aroma. During the process, added enzymes separate the sugar into alcohol and carbon dioxide, causing the mash literally to bubble and boil in the vat. The process ceases when the yeast cells have no more sugar to consume and begin destroying each other.

In the distilling that follows, the alcohol is evaporated out of the mash at a high temperature, then cooled once again into liquid form. The distiller's art consists of maintaining the temperature at just that point where the desired aromatic elements are drawn off with the alcohol, while the unwanted aldehydes and fusel oils are left behind.

There are two distinct distilling methods, each producing a very different grade of rum. The older method employs a simple pot still in which the more aromatic substances are prevented from separating from the alcohol. This method gives us heavy-bodied rums, with an alcohol content of 75 to 80 percent. Heavy-bodied rum is produced almost exclusively on islands that were formerly British, and especially in Jamaica.

Lighter rums are made in a "continuous" still; the distillates escape at differing boiling points and are trapped in separate column stills. With this method, it is easier to exclude the undesirable aromatic substances. Mixing the distillates produces light-bodied rums, which have virtually driven the heavier brands off the market.

Immediately after distillation, rum is unpalatable. It tastes extremely raw, and runs about 75 percent alcohol. At this stage it is commonly known as *aguardiente*, or burning water. Only during the aging period of months or even years do the acids in the distilled liquid combine with the alcohol to form the esters essential for smoothness of flavor.

It is simply the manner of storage that determines whether the rum is finally brown or white. When stored in oak barrels—generally charred on the inside—rum assumes a yellow to brownish cast. Stored in stainless steel tanks, it remains colorless. A rum that is deep brown in color has in all probability been tinted with burnt sugar or caramel.

The rum's ultimate color and strength are determined by the master blender, or *maestro de ron*. It is his responsibility to maintain a consistent quality for the given brand.

REGIONS & VARIETIES

Mexico:
Tequila &
Mescal
Acapulco
Almeca
Arandas
Baja
Beamero
Corrida
Crendain
Don Emilio
Dorado
El Gran Matador
Fonda Blanca
Gavilan
Gusano Rojo
 Mescal
Herradura
José Cuervo
La Prima
Mariachi
Matador
Miguel de la
 Mescal
Monte Alban
 Mescal
Monte Zuma
Old Mexico
Old Mr. Boston
Ole
Olmeca
Pancho Villa
Pepe Lopez
San Matias
Sauza
Souza
Tequila Espuela
Tequila Silla
Two Fingers
Veulo

Brazil:
Cachaça
Pitù
Pinga
Negâ Fulô

Jamaica: Rum
Appleton
Captain Morgan
Caribbean
Columbus
Corona
Coruba
First Rate
Flor de Cabaña
Forgeron
John Canoe
Lemon Hart
Myers's
Parker's Cresta
Red Heart
Robinson

Cuba: Rum
Havana Club

Haiti: Rum
Barbancourt
Champion
Marie Colas
Nazon
Tesserot

Dominican
Republic: Rum
Bermudez

Colombia: Rum
Caldas

Guyana: Rum
Courantin
Demerara

French Guiana:
Rum
Mirande
Prévot

RUM, CACHAÇA, TEQUILA & MESCAL

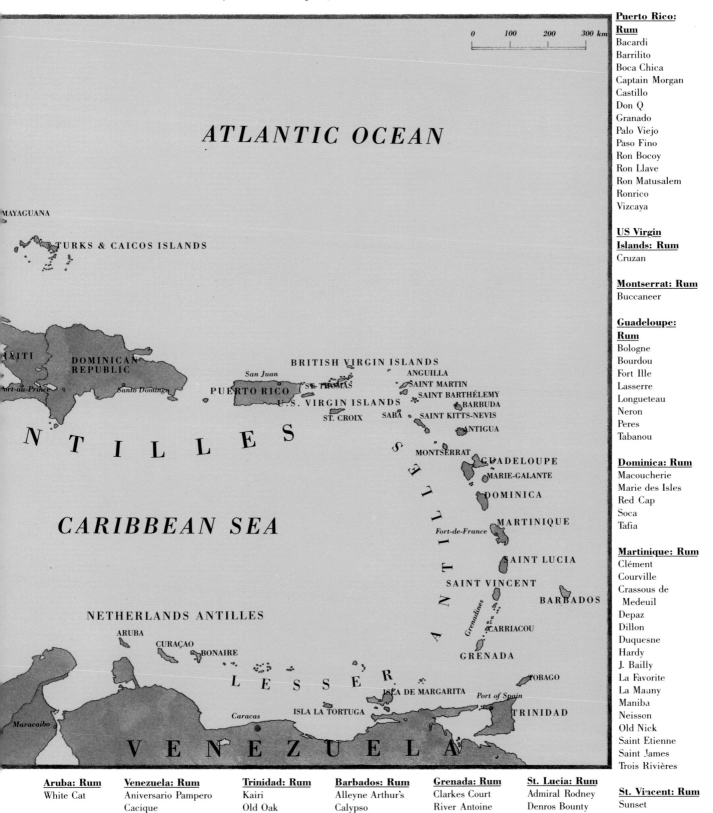

ATLANTIC OCEAN

MAYAGUANA

TURKS & CAICOS ISLANDS

HAITI
DOMINICAN REPUBLIC
Port-au-Prince
Santo Domingo
San Juan
PUERTO RICO
BRITISH VIRGIN ISLANDS
ANGUILLA
ST. THOMAS
SAINT MARTIN
U.S. VIRGIN ISLANDS
SAINT BARTHÉLEMY
ST. CROIX
BARBUDA
SABA
SAINT KITTS-NEVIS
ANTIGUA
MONTSERRAT
GUADELOUPE
MARIE-GALANTE
DOMINICA
MARTINIQUE
Fort-de-France
SAINT LUCIA
SAINT VINCENT
BARBADOS
Grenadines
CARRIACOU
GRENADA

ANTILLES

LESSER ANTILLES

CARIBBEAN SEA

NETHERLANDS ANTILLES
ARUBA
CURAÇAO
BONAIRE

TOBAGO
ISLA DE MARGARITA
Port of Spain
ISLA LA TORTUGA
TRINIDAD
Caracas

Maracaibo

VENEZUELA

0 100 200 300 km

Puerto Rico:
Rum
Bacardi
Barrilito
Boca Chica
Captain Morgan
Castillo
Don Q
Granado
Palo Viejo
Paso Fino
Ron Bocoy
Ron Llave
Ron Matusalem
Ronrico
Vizcaya

**US Virgin
Islands: Rum**
Cruzan

Montserrat: Rum
Buccaneer

Guadeloupe:
Rum
Bologne
Bourdou
Fort Ille
Lasserre
Longueteau
Neron
Peres
Tabanou

Dominica: Rum
Macoucherie
Marie des Isles
Red Cap
Soca
Tafia

Martinique: Rum
Clément
Courville
Crassous de
  Medeuil
Depaz
Dillon
Duquesne
Hardy
J. Bailly
La Favorite
La Mauny
Maniba
Neisson
Old Nick
Saint Etienne
Saint James
Trois Rivières

St. Vincent: Rum
Sunset

Aruba: Rum
White Cat

Venezuela: Rum
Aniversario Pampero
Cacique

Trinidad: Rum
Kairi
Old Oak

Barbados: Rum
Alleyne Arthur's
Calypso
Cockspur
Goddard's
Mount Gay

Grenada: Rum
Clarkes Court
River Antoine
Sipper

St. Lucia: Rum
Admiral Rodney
Denros Bounty

Cuba

In 1793, the Spaniard Don Francisco de Arango y Parreño laid out Cuba's first large sugarcane plantations, designed to be worked by slaves. This was the beginning of what became for a long time the greatest sugar industry in the world. And, it was the beginning of Cuba's rum production.

Over the next few decades, Cuban rum producers worked to develop new and better ways of distilling rum best suited for export, the type that is still considered typically Cuban. It is a light and especially pure rum, distilled from molasses that has been laced with specially cultivated yeasts and repeatedly filtered through either charcoal or sand. By the mid-nineteenth century, Cuban rum had conquered the world market, and only a short time later the island's most famous distiller began production. On February 4, 1862, the Spaniard Don Facundo Bacardi paid $3,500 for a rum distillery in Santiago and set about creating a distilling process that would produce an especially light rum that could be drunk straight. Don Facundo is remembered in Cuba not only for his famous Bacardi rum, but also because he was a champion of independence from Spain. His political activities brought him a few years of exile on an island off the coast of Africa, but after the liberation of Cuba, he became the mayor of Santiago.

Like the other rum producers in Cuba, the Bacardi firm profited greatly from U.S. Prohibition during the twenties. To meet the growing demand for rum in the United States, Bacardi began distilling in Mexico as well as Cuba in 1930, and in Puerto Rico in 1935. When the Cuban rum industry was nationalized by Fidel Castro in 1960, Bacardi moved its headquarters to the Puerto Rican plant.

The Cuban government has meanwhile reorganized the rum industry and given it new stimulus. On the former Bacardi property a whole new plant has been constructed, one with an annual production of 30 million liters and a total area of 1½ million square feet. With storage space for 200,000 oak barrels, this is the largest rum distillery in the world.

Today's Cuban rum—marketed as "Havana Club," a brand name that dates back to 1878—is produced in two traditional Cuban flavors. There is the lighter *carta blanca*, a white rum used in the more familiar Cuban cocktails, and *carta oro*, a heavier type colored with caramel. Though sweeter, this darker variety can still be considered dry.

Then, of course, there is *añejo*, a choice variety aged an extra long time, which is the pride of every distillery.

Puerto Rico

It is thought that the first Caribbean rum was produced in Puerto Rico, an island belonging to the Greater Antilles. Puerto Rico's first governor, Ponce de Léon, constructed a distillery shortly after his arrival there in 1508. Today, with its fourteen highly mechanized distilleries, Puerto Rico is the largest rum producer in the world. Eight percent of the rum imported into the United States comes from this island. Puerto Rico's distillers owe their preeminence over other Caribbean exporters to the special trade advantages they enjoy, for Puerto Rican products are imported into the United States duty-free. The is-

land's inhabitants have been U.S. citizens since 1917, and since 1952 Puerto Rico has been a self-governing commonwealth of the United States.

Puerto Rico's distilleries are located across the entire island. This means that given the island's great geographic diversity, some distilleries are situated in dry regions, others in rainy ones, and accordingly, the sugarcane they process varies given these diverse conditions. Furthermore, each producer breeds his own special yeasts. As a result, any brand of Puerto Rican rum, though distilled from molasses in continuous stills, may differ greatly from any other. Most of it, however, may be classed as light and dry.

Thanks in large part to its rum production, Puerto Rico has become the most prosperous state in the Caribbean. Its government funds a special research distillery at the University of Puerto Rico, an indication of the importance of rum for the island's economy.

The largest distillery belongs to the Bacardi firm, originally from Cuba, which also operates in Mexico, Spain, Brazil, Venezuela, Martinique, and Bermuda. The Puerto Rican Ronrico distillery has a capacity of over 100,000 barrels and is famous for its mature rum, aged for more than six years.

Jamaica

In the nineteenth century, there were over a thousand rum distilleries in Jamaica, many of them, admittedly, quite small. Only seven major ones continue to produce today. Jamaican rum has fared badly on the world market; even a century ago it failed to suit the tastes of the majority of consumers. Originally produced exclusively in simple pot stills, it is traditionally quite heavy; its strong flavor is also a result of the delayed fermentation typically employed. Indeed its flavor is so strong, researchers tell us, that when only a cubic centimeter of rum is dissolved in a hundred liters of water one can still taste it.

Called high-continental or German-flavored, these Jamaican varieties are ideally suited for blending and therefore meet with a certain degree of success in importing countries. Those who prefer to drink their rum undiluted have turned increasingly to the lighter varieties, but even so, Jamaican rum has always enjoyed a worldwide reputation, and there continue to be connoisseurs who prize its characteristic strength and aroma.

Jamaica's distillers have recently changed certain traditional procedures. Some now employ the continuous still, producing a light rum known as Common Clean. One can also occasionally find lighter varieties produced by the old pot still process, and especially for the English market there is a medium rum. The latter, traditionally designated Home Trade quality, comes in two varieties, each still bearing the name of a plantation owner from the eighteenth century: Wedderburn and Plummer. Both of these are slow-fermented, medium heavy rums, Plummer being the less aromatic of the two.

Traditionally, and even today, most of the rum produced in Jamaica is shipped in the barrel to London, where it is then aged and bottled. The two best known Jamaican brands are Appleton, which has been distilled in the country's capital of Kingston since 1825, and the popular Myers's.

Martinique, Guadeloupe, and Haiti

The French drink more rum than any other liquor, and naturally most of it comes from the French Antilles. Since 1946, the French Caribbean islands of Martinique and Guadeloupe have belonged to the European Common Market, but despite this tariff advantage, any French dream of conquering the European market with its Caribbean rums has not come true. The rums of Martinique and Guadeloupe have distinct character and are an acquired taste.

Most of the rum imported by France comes from the many distilleries on Martinique, which have a combined annual production of over four million gallons. Roughly half of this rum is only 50 proof and is distilled directly from the sap of the sugarcane.

Martinique's colorless rums, known as *grappe blanche* or *rhum agricole*, are aged in stainless steel vats. They are the basis for the famous Punch de la Martinique, a mixture of rum, sugar syrup, and lime juice that is sold not only in bars, but also all over the countryside. On the other hand, *rhum Saint James*, distilled from sugarcane syrup and a large amount of dunder, is dark brown and very aromatic.

Though not so well known abroad, rum made from molasses continues to be produced by a number of distilleries adjacent to Martinique's defunct sugar refineries. Martinique's rums made from molasses

and sold under the designation *grand arome* tend to be heavy and strong, for they are allowed to ferment a long time, from eight to twelve days.

The finest French Caribbean rum is *rhum Clement*, which is bottled in both its white and colored forms. The best brands have been aged in the barrel for up to twelve years.

Haiti was a colony of France only until 1793, but it has kept to the French method of making rum from sugarcane syrup to the present day. Haitian rum producers have traditionally employed the pot still and distilled twice. A quantity of the rum from the first distillation is not exported but sold in Haiti itself. Colorless and quite strong, it is marketed under the name Clairin.

Haiti's most famous export rum is Barbancourt, whose producers boast that the sugarcane they use is grown in soil with the same proportion of lime and sediment as that of the best wine regions of France, namely Cognac and Champagne.

Elsewhere in the Caribbean and the world

In recent years the Barbadian rum Mount Gay (a map of Barbados appears on its label) has become the choice of the jet set and the Caribbean yacht crowd. To meet the growing demand for Mount Gay, both in its white and colored forms, Barbados has increased production enormously. The porous soil of this island, composed of lime, coral sand, and volcanic ash, is especially good for growing sugarcane and many of the island's brands owe their characteristic flavor to the addition of plums to the mash.

Other islands in the Lesser Antilles—Antigua, Montserrat, St. Kitts, Nevis, Dominica, St. Lucia, St. Vincent and the Grenadines, Grenada—also produce a certain amount of rum, as do the Dutch islands off the coast of Venezuela. Most of it is quite strong and rather crude, and the total output is so small that most of it is consumed locally. Trinidad distills more rum than the other islands, and it is sold under the general designation, Antilles rum. This Trinidadian product is light and delicate in flavor.

The U.S. Virgin Islands, an island group to the north of the Lesser Antilles, is a veritable giant in the rum industry. Fully 15 percent of the rum consumed in the United States is produced there and most of it is exported in the barrel. Like Puerto Rico, these islands enjoy a distinct tariff advantage inasmuch as they belong to the U.S. trading community. The rum they produce is somewhat heavier than Puerto Rico's; St. Croix exports an especially robust rum under the name Cruzan.

Another important exporter of rum lies to the south, on the South American mainland. Guyana, formerly a British colony, continues to be the chief producer of the rum drunk in England and Canada, for reasons clearly linked to its history. Its best-known brand is Demarara, named after the river valley which grows most of Guyana's sugarcane. Demarara is dark brown in color, due to the addition of caramel, and so resembles the heaviest of Jamaican rums. However, since the molasses is permitted to ferment only a short time, it is lighter than the Jamaican varieties. This Guyanese brand is often referred to simply as Navy rum, for since the seventeenth century, every sailor in the British Royal Navy has had the right to his daily ration of Demarara. In Guyana itself, however, the addition of various fruits and seasonings make brands such as Courantin more appealing to local taste. Rum is also distilled in neighboring French Guiana and in Venezuela.

For that matter, there are distillers in nearly all tropical countries where sugarcane is grown. Réunion, for example, an overseas department of France close to Madagascar in the Indian Ocean, produces a considerable quantity of relatively high quality rum. Rum from Réunion is colorless, and is aged only a short time. Connoisseurs also prize two brands of rum from the Philippines, Tanduay and Panay.

In East Asia, the original homeland of sugarcane, a liquor similar to rum is distilled from molasses and other native ingredients. This is the well-known arrack, "the rum of the Asiatics." Arrack is the general term for any liquor whose flavor comes from the sap, leaves, or fruit of the palm tree; there are also varieties made from figs. Batavia, the most famous arrack, comes from Java, and is made from molasses, rice, and palm sap—sometimes a fermented palm sap known as *toddy*. In addition to Java, the chief producers of arrack are Thailand, India, and Sri Lanka.

There is only one spot in the world where rum is distilled but no sugarcane is grown. This is in Massachusetts, in New England. These rum distilleries were part of the notorious "three-cornered trade" of the late eighteenth century, exchanging molasses, rum, and slaves between New England, Africa, and the Caribbean colonies. The Massachusetts distilleries, which now produce an annual 200,000 gallons of heavy, aromatic rum from West Indian molasses, are historical anomalies, holdovers from the heyday of the sugarcane and rum trade that left its mark on the Caribbean more than anywhere else.

EQUIPMENT

For most mixed drinks you will need a shaker, preferably a professional one—called an American or Boston shaker—made of crystal and stainless steel. Important: always place the ice in the shaker first, then any nonalcoholic ingredients, and finally the alcohol.

A strainer is required to keep the ice out of the drink as it is poured. Its spiral spring allows it to conform to any size shaker or glass.

For stirred drinks you will need a tall stirring glass and a bar spoon.

A traditional jigger holds 1½ ounces; the measure of a pony is typically 1 ounce.

Other utensils required in any bar are a container for ice, together with ice tongs and a scoop, a bar knife with a corkscrew, a bottle opener, cocktail skewers, a nutmeg grater, a cutting board and paring knife for fruit, straws, and a clamp stopper for opened champagne.

It is also essential that a tropical bar have an electric blender. With it you can create the thick, cold mixture of ice, liquor, and juices that is so popular in hot climates—also in northern latitudes, to be sure, but less so. A blender is indispensable when combining fresh fruits with liquor and ice. First pour in the liquid ingredients, then the crushed ice, and finally the slices of fruit. Let the blender run first on low speed for roughly five seconds, then switch to high speed for another fifteen to twenty seconds. Then pour the ice-cold mixture directly into a cocktail glass without using a strainer.

GLASSWARE

(1) Small cocktail glass, (2) cocktail or champagne glass, (3) champagne flute, (4) sherry glass, (5) whiskey sour glass, (6) old fashioned glass, (7) highball glass, (8) tall drink glass, (9) small glass for exotic drinks, (10) large glass for exotic drinks, (11) heatproof punch glass.

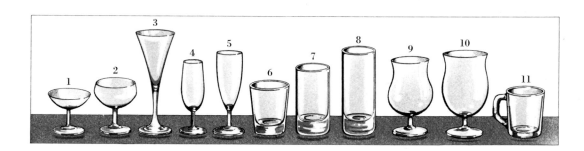

WINES

In your tropical bar you will need to have sherry (dry, medium, and sweet), vermouth (dry and sweet), and Dubonnet.

LIQUEURS

Triple sec or Cointreau, Tia Maria, Kahlúa, Southern Comfort, amaretto, Galliano, crème de cassis, crème de menthe (green and white), crème de bananes, crème de cacao (white and brown), apricot brandy, and Cherry Heering.

SPIRITS

Most important, of course, is rum. You will need a white, a golden, and a brown—all 80 proof—as well as a high-proof rum (151 proof). Next you need tequila, both clear and light brown, mescal, and cachaça.

JUICES

Fresh lemon juice; Rose's Lime Juice; canned, unsweetened pineapple juice; fresh orange juice; tomato juice; and the juices of the tropical fruits maracuja (also known as passion fruit), mango, papaya, and the various Annonas; coconut cream and milk.

SYRUPS

Grenadine, maracuja, banana, mango, lime, raspberry, strawberry, bilberry. Also almond, mint, and sugar syrups.

MIXERS

Tonic water, cola, and soda water.

FRESH FRUITS AND FLAVORINGS

Mangoes, oranges, lemons, limes, papayas, passion fruit, cherimoya, and pineapple.

Tabasco, Worcestershire sauce, Angostura bitters. Green and black olives, maraschino cherries, pepper, salt, celery salt, nutmeg, sugar cubes, eggs, and cream.

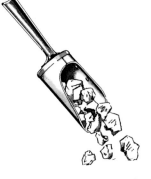

MIXING BASICS
Tropical drinks, with the exception of punches and grogs, of course, must always be served ice cold. The rule of thumb for ice is the colder the better, as colder ice is slower to melt and so does not water down the drink much.

In many recipes it is recommended that a drink be mixed "in a shaker with crushed ice." Normally, this ensures that the drink will be cold enough. When pouring into cocktail glasses, you  need to watch that no bits of ice slip into the drink. For those who wish their drinks colder still, you can always place a cone of fresh crushed ice in the cocktail glass and pour the drink over it.

 Stirred drinks that are to be served without ice are mixed in a stirring glass with a great deal of ice, then strained. You should always use ice cubes in a stirring glass, never crushed ice. The general rule is that you reach for the stirring glass to mix very fluid drinks consisting of easily blended ingredients.

The shaker is used for nearly all drinks containing ingredients not easily blended, such as juices, cream, milk, eggs, or syrups. Shake the mixture vigorously for ten to twenty seconds. If you shake it longer the drink will be watery from the melting ice. Stirred drinks remain clear; shaken ones become cloudy.

When pouring from either a shaker or a stirring glass, do not pour all of the liquid at once, but in two or three stages. This ensures that everything is truly well blended.

Drinks served with soda must be stirred with a long bar spoon.

For many drinks it is essential that the glass itself be ice cold. Glasses may be chilled in the refrigerator—better yet in the freezer.

*V*oy a tomar otro de estos grandes sin azúcar," he said to Serafín.

"*En seguida, Don Tomás,*" Serafín said. "Are you going to try to beat the record?"

"No. I'm just drinking with calmness."

"You were drinking with calmness when you set the record," Serafín said. "With calmness and fortitude from morning until night. And you walked out on your own feet."

"The hell with the record."

"You've got a chance to break it," Serafín told him. "Drinking as you are now and eating a little as you go along, you have an excellent chance."

"Tom, try to break the record," Honest Lil said. "I'm here as a witness."

"He doesn't need any witness," Serafín said. "I'm the witness. When I go off I'll give the count to Constante. You're further along right now than you were the day you set the record."

"The hell with the record."

"You're in good form. You're drinking well and steady and they're not having any effect on you."

"Fuck the record."

"All right. *Como usted quiere.* I'm keeping count just in case you change your mind."

"He'll keep count all right," Honest Lil said. "He has the duplicate tickets."

"What do you want, woman? Do you want a real record or a phoney record?"

"Neither. I want a *highbalito* with *agua mineral.*"

"*Como siempre,*" Serafín said. . . .

I do feel better, Thomas Hudson thought. That is the funny part. You always feel better and you always get over your remorse. There's only one thing you don't get over and that is death.

"You ever been dead?" he said to Lil.

"Of course not."

"*Yo tampoco.*"

"Why did you say that? You scare me when you talk like that."

"I don't mean to scare you, honey. I

don't want to scare anybody ever."

"I like it when you call me honey."

This isn't getting anywhere, Thomas Hudson thought. Isn't there anything else you could do that would produce the same effect rather than sit with beat-up old Honest Lil in La Floridita at the old tarts' end of the bar and get drunk? If you only have four days couldn't you employ them better? Where?, he thought. At Alfred's Sin House? You're doing all right where you are. The drinking couldn't be any better, nor as good, anywhere in the world and you're down to the drinking now, kid, and you better get just as far in it as you can. That's what you've got now and you better like it and like it on all frequencies. You know you always liked it and you loved it and it's what you have now, so you better love it.

"I love it," he said out loud.

"What!"

"Drinking. Not just drinking. Drinking these double frozens without sugar. If you drank that many with sugar it would make you sick."

"*Ya lo creo*. And if anybody else drank that many without sugar they'd be dead."

"Maybe I'll be dead."

"No, you won't. You'll just break the record and then we'll go to my place and you'll go to sleep and the worst thing that will happen is if you snore."

"Did I snore last time?"

"*Horrores*. And you called me by about ten different names in the night."

"I'm sorry."

"No. I thought it was funny. I learned two or three things I didn't know. Don't your other girls ever get upset when you call them by so many different names?"

"I haven't any other girls. Just a wife."

"I try hard to like her and think well of her but it is very difficult. Naturally I never let anyone speak against her."

"I'll speak against her."

"No. Don't. That is vulgar. I hate two things. Men when they cry. I know they have to cry. But I don't like it. And I hate to hear them speak against their wives. Yet they nearly all do. So don't you do it, because we are having such a lovely time."

"Good. The hell with her. We won't speak about her."

"Please, Tom. You know I think she is very beautiful. She is. Really. *Pero no es mujer para ti.* But let us not speak against her."

"Right."

"Tell me another happy story. It doesn't even have to have love in it if it makes you happy to tell it."

"I don't think I know any happy stories."

"Don't be like that. You know thousands. Take another drink and tell me a happy story."

"Why don't you do some of the work?"

"What work?"

"The goddamned morale building."

"*Tú tienes la moral muy baja.*"

"Sure. I'm well aware of it. But why don't you tell a few stories to build it up?"

"You have to do it yourself. You know that. I'll do anything else you want me to. You know that."

"OK," Thomas Hudson said. "You really want another happy story?"

"Please. There's your drink. One more happy story and one more drink and you'll feel good."

"You guarantee it?"

"No," she said and she began to cry again as she looked up at him, crying easily and naturally as water wells up in a spring. "Tom, why can't you tell me what's the matter? I'm afraid to ask now. Is that it?"

"That's it," Thomas Hudson said. Then she began to cry hard and he had to put his arm around her and try to comfort her with all of the people there at the bar. She was not crying beautifully now. She was crying straight and destructively.

"Oh my poor Tom," she said. "Oh my poor Tom."

"Pull yourself together, *mujer*, and drink a brandy. Now we are going to be cheerful."

"Oh, I don't want to be cheerful now. I'll never be cheerful again."

"Look," Thomas Hudson said. "You see how much good it does to tell people things?"

"I'll be cheerful," she said. "Just give me a minute. I'll go out to the ladies and I'll be all right."

You damned well better be, Thomas Hudson thought. Because I'm feeling really bad and if you don't quit crying, or if you talk about it, I'll pull the hell out of here. And if I pull the hell out of here where the hell else have I got to go? He was aware of the limitations, and no one's Sin House was the answer.

"Give me another double frozen daiquiri without sugar. *No sé lo que pasa con esta mujer.*"

"She cries like a sprinkling can," the barman said. "They ought to have her instead of the aqueduct."

"How's the aqueduct coming?" Thomas Hudson asked.

The man next to him on his left at the bar, a short, cheerful-faced man with a broken nose whose face he knew well but whose name and whose politics escaped him said, "Those *cabrones*. They can always get money for water since water is the one great necessity. Everything else is necessary. But water there is no substitute for and you cannot do without some water. So they can always get money to bring water. So there will never be a proper aqueduct."

"I'm not sure I follow you completely."

"*Sí, hombre.* They can always get money for an aqueduct because an aqueduct is absolutely necessary. Therefore they cannot afford an aqueduct. Would you kill the goose that lays the golden aqueduct?"

"Why not build the aqueduct and make some money out of it and find another *truco?*"

"There's no trick like water. You can always get money for the promise to produce water. No politician would destroy a *truco* like that by building an adequate aqueduct. Aspirant politicians occasionally shoot one another in the lowest levels of politics. But no politician would so strike at the true basis of political economy. Let me propose a toast to the Custom House, a lottery racket, the free numbers racket, the fixed price of sugar, and the eternal lack of an aqueduct."

"*Prosit*," Thomas Hudson said.

"You're not German, are you?"

"No. American."

"Then let us drink to Roosevelt, Churchill, Batista, and the lack of an aqueduct."

"To Stalin."

"Certainly. To Stalin, Central Hershey, marijuana, and the lack of an aqueduct."

"To Adolphe Luque."

"To Adolphe Luque, to Adolf Hitler, to Philadelphia, to Gene Tunney, to Key West, and to the lack of an aqueduct."

Honest Lil came in to the bar from the ladies room while they were talking. She had repaired her face and she was not crying but you could see she had been hit.

"Do you know this gentleman?" Thomas Hudson said to her, introducing his new friend, or his old friend newly found.

"Only in bed," the gentleman said.

"*Cállate*," Honest Lil said. "He's a politician," she explained to Thomas Hudson. "*Muy hambriento en este momento.*"

"Thirsty," the politician corrected. "And at your orders," he said to Thomas Hudson. "What will you have?"

"A double frozen daiquiri without sugar. Should we roll for them?"

"No. Let me buy them. I have unlimited credit here."

"He's a good man," Honest Lil said to Thomas Hudson in a whisper while the other was attracting the attention of the nearest barman. "A politician. But very honest and very cheerful."

The man put his arm around Lil. "You're thinner every day, *mi vida*," he said. "We must belong to the same political party."

"To the aqueduct," Thomas Hudson said.

"My God, no. What are you trying to do? Take the bread out of our mouths and put water in?"

"Let's drink to when the *puta guerra* will finish," Lil said.

"Drink."

"To the black market," the man said. "To the cement shortage. To those who control the supply of black beans."

"Drink," Thomas Hudson said and

added, "To rice."

"To rice," the politician said. "Drink."

"Do you feel better?" Honest Lil asked.

"Sure."

He looked at her and saw she was going to start to cry again.

"You cry again," he said, "and I'll break your jaw."

There was a lithographed poster behind the bar of a politician in white suit and the slogan *"Un Alcalde Mejor,"* a better mayor. It was a big poster and the better mayor stared straight into the eyes of every drinker.

"To *Un Alcalde Peor,"* the politician said. "To A Worse Mayor."

"Will you run?" Thomas Hudson asked him.

"Absolutely."

"That's wonderful," Honest Lil said. "Let's draw up our platform."

"It isn't difficult," the candidate said. *"Un Alcalde Peor.* We've got a winning slogan. What do we need a platform for?"

"We ought to have a platform," Lil said. "Don't you think so, Tomás?"

"I think so. What about Down with the Rural Schools?"

"Down," said the candidate.

"Menos guaguas y peores," Honest Lil suggested.

"Good. Fewer and worse buses."

"Why not do away with transport entirely?" suggested the candidate. *"Es más sencillo."*

"Okay," Thomas Hudson said. *"Cero transporte."*

"Short and noble," the candidate said. "And it shows we are impartial. But we could elaborate it. What about *Cero transporte aéreo, terrestre, y marítimo?"*

"Wonderful. We're getting a real platform. How do we stand on leprosy?"

"Por una lepra más grande para Cuba," said the candidate.

"Por el cáncer cubano," Thomas Hudson said.

"Por una tuberculosis ampliada, adecuada, y permanente par Cuba y los cubanos," said the candidate. "That's a little bit long but it will sound good on the radio. Where do we stand on syphilis, my coreligionists?"

"Por una sífilis criolla cien por cien."

"Good," said the candidate. "Down with *Penicilina* and other tricks of *Yanqui* Imperialism."

"Down," said Thomas Hudson.

"It seems to me as though we ought to drink something," Honest Lil said. "How does it seem to you, *correligionarios?"*

"A magnificent idea," said the candidate. "Who but you could have had an idea like that?"

"You," Honest Lil said.

"Attack my credit," the candidate said. "Let's see how my credit stands up under really heavy fire. Bar-chap, bar-fellow, boy: the same all round. And for this political associate of mine: without sugar."

"That's an idea for a slogan," Honest Lil said. "Cuba's Sugar for Cubans."

"Down with the Colossus of the North," Thomas Hudson said.

"Down," repeated the others.

"We need more domestic slogans, more municipal slogans. We shouldn't get too much into the international field while we are fighting a war and are still allies."

"Still I think we ought to Down the Colossus of the North," Thomas Hudson said. "It's really an ideal time while the Colossus is fighting a global war. I think we ought to down him."

"We'll down him after I'm elected."

"To *Un Alcalde Peor*," Thomas Hudson said.

"To All of Us. To the party," the Alcalde Peor said. He raised his glass.

"We must remember the circumstances of the founding of the party and write out the manifesto. What's the date anyway?"

"The twentieth. More or less."

"The twentieth of what?"

"The twentieth more or less of February. *El grito de La Floridita.*"

"It's a solemn moment," Thomas Hudson said. "Can you write, Honest Lil? Can you perpetuate all this?"

"I can write. But I can't write right now."

"There are a few more problems we have to take a stand on," the Alcalde Peor said. "Listen, Colossus of the North, why don't you buy this round? You've seen how valiant my credit is and how he stands up

to the attack. But there's no need to kill the poor bird when we know he's losing. Come on, Colossus."

"Don't call me Colossus. We're against the damn Colossus."

"All right, governor. What do you do, anyway?"

"I'm a scientist."

"*Sobre todo en la cama,*" Honest Lil said. "He made extensive studies in China."

"Well, whatever you are, buy this one," the Alcalde Peor said. "And let's get on with the platform."

"What about the Home?"

"A sacred subject. The Home enjoys equal dignity with religion. We must be careful and subtle. What about this: *Abajo los padres de familias?*"

"It has dignity. But why not just: Down with the Home?"

"*Abajo el Home.* It's a beautiful sentiment but many might confuse it with *béisbol.*"

"What about Little Children?"

"Suffer them to come unto me once they are of electoral age," said the Alcalde Peor.

"What about divorce?" Thomas Hudson asked.

"Another touchy problem," the Alcalde Peor said. "*Bastante espinoso.* How do you feel about divorce?"

"Perhaps we shouldn't take up divorce. It conflicts with our campaign in favour of the Home."

"All right, let's drop it. Now let me see—"

"You can't," Honest Lil said. "You're cockeyed."

"Don't criticize me, woman," the Alcalde Peor told her. "One thing we must do."

"What?"

"*Orinar.*"

"I agree," Thomas Hudson heard himself saying. "It is basic."

"As basic as the lack of the aqueduct. It is founded on water."

"It's founded on alcohol."

"Only a small percentage in comparison with the water. Water is the basic thing. You are a scientist. What percentage of water are we composed of?"

"Eighty-seven and three-tenths," said Thomas Hudson, taking a chance and knowing he was wrong.

"Exactly," said the Alcalde Peor. "Should we go while we can still move?"

O ne cannot make a good Daiquiri without a good rum, without limes and a fine sugar!"

The original daiquiri, like many classic cocktails, contains but three ingredients: rum, lime juice, and sugar. The lime juice should be squeezed fresh for each drink, but if necessary, fresh lemon juice can be substituted—never, however, a lemon concentrate. For fruit daiquiris follow the same rule; never try to substitute a concentrate, syrup, or commercial juice for the real fresh fruit.

As with many famous drinks, there is a legend about the origin of the daiquiri. Tradition has it that it was invented near the end of the nineteenth century by two engineers, Pagliuchi and Cox, working at a copper mine in the Cuban province of Oriente. They wanted to serve something to some guests, but had nothing in their canteen but rum, limes, sugar, and ice. The resultant cocktail proved highly satisfying, and Pagliuchi is supposed to have exclaimed: "Let's just call it a 'Daiquiri'!"—a logical suggestion, for that was the name of the closest village.

Constante Ribailagua, the head bartender in Havana's legendary La Floridita bar from 1912 to 1952, and to many the king of cocktails, is said to have mixed more than ten million daiquiris over his forty-year reign. He himself invented a number of drinks, most notably the popular Frozen Daiquiri, and La Floridita indeed came to be known as *La Catedral del Daiquiri*. Anyone who knows something of the bar scene during the twenties and thirties—the professionalism, pride, high standards, obsessiveness, and worldwide renown of Cuba's bartenders—will appreciate what it meant for Ribailagua to be singled out for such an honor.

Ribailagua was a perfectionist. It is said, for example, that he had an assistant give his limes a preliminary kneading after which he would then roll them against his cutting board again himself, so that none of their juice would be lost. In 1927, an English journalist wrote admiringly: "It is worth a trip to Havana just to watch Constante at work."

DAIQUIRI NATURAL*

1 scoop crushed ice

juice of ½ lime

2 teaspoons sugar or sugar syrup

1¾ oz. white rum

Mix vigorously in a shaker. Serve in an iced cocktail glass.
*Original version from 1898

CHARLES DAIQUIRI   *1980

1 scoop crushed ice

juice of 1 lime

2 teaspoons sugar

¾ oz. Cointreau

1½ oz. white rum

¾ oz. brown rum

Mix in a shaker. Serve in a large cocktail glass with a lime twist.

LA FLORIDITA DAIQUIRI

1 scoop crushed ice

juice of 1 lime

2 teaspoons sugar or sugar syrup

¼ oz. maraschino

1¾ oz. white rum

Mix in a shaker. Serve in an iced cocktail glass. (You may substitute Cointreau for maraschino.)

FLORIDA DAIQUIRI

1 scoop crushed ice

juice of ½ lime

2 teaspoons sugar

¼ oz. grapefruit juice

¼ oz. maraschino

1¾ oz. white rum

Mix in a shaker. Serve in a cocktail glass or champagne flute.

FROZEN DAIQUIRI*

1 scoop crushed ice

juice of ½ lime

2 teaspoons sugar

1¾ oz. white rum

Mix in a blender. Serve in a cocktail glass or champagne flute.
*Coldest version of the Daiquiri

PINK DAIQUIRI

1 scoop crushed ice

juice of ½ lime

1 teaspoon sugar

2 splashes grenadine

1¾ oz. white rum

Mix in a shaker. Serve in a cocktail glass.

FRENCH DAIQUIRI

Follow the recipe for Pink Daiquiri, substituting crème de cassis for grenadine.

BANANA DAIQUIRI

1 scoop crushed ice

½ banana

juice of ¼ lime

1 teaspoon sugar

1¾ oz. white rum

Mix in a blender. Serve in a large cocktail glass or champagne flute. (I add 2 to 3 drops banana syrup.)

PINEAPPLE DAIQUIRI

1 scoop crushed ice

1 slice of pineapple

juice of ¼ lime

1 teaspoon sugar

1¾ oz. white rum

Mix in a blender. Serve in a large cocktail glass or champagne flute.

PEACH DAIQUIRI

1 scoop crushed ice

½ peach, peeled

juice of ¼ lime

1 teaspoon sugar

1¾ oz. white rum

Mix in a blender. Serve in a large cocktail glass or champagne flute.

STRAWBERRY DAIQUIRI

1 scoop crushed ice

3 or 4 strawberries

juice of ¼ lime

1 to 2 teaspoons sugar

1¾ oz. white rum

Mix in a blender. Serve in a large cocktail glass or champagne flute.

MINT DAIQUIRI

1 scoop crushed ice

3 or 4 mint leaves, to taste

juice of ½ lime

2 teaspoons sugar

2 splashes Cointreau

1¾ oz. white rum

Mix in a blender. Serve in a large cocktail glass or champagne flute. (Since mint has a very intense flavor, use only a few leaves. Let the blender run somewhat longer than usual.)

DERBY-ORANGE DAIQUIRI

1 scoop crushed ice

juice of 1 orange

juice of ¼ lime

1 teaspoon sugar

1¾ oz. white rum

Mix in a blender. Serve in a large cocktail glass or champagne flute.

Farida and Roberto sat like two defendants in the bus which, halting and squeaking, turned onto the main road from Oranjestad to St. Nicolaas. Anyone could see in one glance the reason for their manner: while Roberto had wooly, curly hair and skin the color of ebony, Farida's hair was light and wavy, and her complexion was like coffee lightened with cream. Seemingly insensible to the "witty" jokes and nasty remarks their fellow passengers tossed their way, they stared out the window silently, their hands intertwined.

When the bus stopped at the Santa Cruz Bar, Roberto gave Farida a hasty kiss on her cheek before she dashed off the bus, looking only straight ahead. Roberto sighed loudly.

Why were mothers so unreasonable? Farida's mother didn't want to know anything about their relationship, which had already been simmering for a year. Often enough she had impressed upon her daughter the need "to raise" her color. Roberto was a nice enough man, made a decent living as a civil servant, but marriage to him meant a setback on the way to becoming white. True, according to Arubian standards, Farida was already an old maid at twenty-one years, but she could and should still hook a white man: if not an Arubian, then at least a Dutch policeman or someone like that. Was it so selfish to take care that at least her grandchildren could be accepted in this white world? It was a white world, Farida knew that, didn't she? . . . And besides, could one honestly believe that a person from a noble Indian race could commit oneself to the descendant of an African slave? Roberto knew that argument by heart by now.

Every Saturday he met Farida at the Aruba Trading Co., and when he carefully hinted at marriage she started whining the litany of maternal objections! They had once nearly gotten into an argument, for he had remarked that, in his opinion, she was too much dominated by her mother. "But she is my Mother, *mi Mama*," Farida had exclaimed indignantly and a trifle pathetically.

She then threw it up to him that their Saturday meetings were only possible because she—on his suggestion—had made her mother believe that she was taking a course in business correspondence at the Juliana School so that she might later be able to earn more money to help support the family. (Her mother had shaken her head at this, declaring that money was of no importance, but that she wouldn't interfere in her daughter's education.)

He then remarked, flippantly, that everything was fair in love and war. But, in fact, he could be more understanding, for after all, out of love for him, she had deceived—yes, deceived—her mother,

the woman who had given birth to her.

He touched her fingers for just a moment when she handed him her textbook and he smiled at her encouragingly. While she spooned up her enormous banana split, he carefully took her letter out of the book and exchanged it for his own. This weekly ritual meant the end of their tête-à-tête. She was never at ease, for in every patron she thought she recognized someone who would feel obliged to enlighten her mother as to her love escapade.

When she became so frightened, or gave him "that look" when he stroked her hands, he wanted to explain to her that something drastic would have to happen. For he read in her letters that she was by now longing for a relationship that reflected the love stories she devoured at night, trembling with passion, while her blessedly ignorant mother bored the neighbors with endless stories about her daughter's studious nature.

The bus driver blasted his horn by way of greeting an oncoming car, rudely disturbing Roberto's reverie. Instinctively he groped at her letter in his breast pocket and guessed it to be six pages long. Touching hands, a secretive kiss, pages filled with calligraphy in the style of Hogenboom and Moerman—some love affair, he thought bitterly.

The bus stopped with a jolt at the fence of the Lago, Aruba's oil refinery. He watched the workers in their colorful safety helmets file out. A lot of them went straight to the local bar, laughing loudly. They all looked so happy, so carefree, while they probably had more problems than he. With some difficulty he refused the persistent invitation of a friend to go and drink a beer. He still had a long way to walk in the blistering sun. And the sun became more unbearable the closer he came to home, because he knew what would be in store for him there. He would hear once again from his mother how he was too good for a girl who didn't even know who to call "Daddy."

Can you insult your father—may he rest in peace—in that way? He'll turn over in his grave. It is true you are black, but you are "white black." Your mother isn't just anybody. She took care to see that you were born decently, with a midwife and everything that comes with that. And you never slept on a rug, there was always a bed. That last insinuation always made Roberto angry because his mother assumed Farida, who had a number of brothers and sisters, wouldn't have had a bed to sleep in.

He saw his mother's broad figure standing by the table when he entered. She was pressing the *funchi* flat between two plates. Now the crying will start, he thought. He would again have to comfort her and testify to his filial devotion. He was surprised when instead he heard her voice ominously proclaim, "I will stop this

eyebrows. She had started business speaking in Spanish—she came from the Dominican Republic—but she discovered quickly that it was better to use French, for her clients stood in great awe of Haiti, which was generally considered the Mecca for everything paranormal. Any person who came from there could wrap herself in a veil of secrecy and be considered *"nourri dans le serail."* Madushi's French was limited to *"parlez moi de ça"* and *"à la vôtre,"* but her clients, who explained their problems in emotional tirades, didn't know that. "Hispaniola," she always answered when a nosy customer asked her the precise whereabouts of her birthplace, and thus cunningly ducked the impertinent question.

Madushi's practices were known far and wide. She was proud of the fact that all her clients could count on the fulfillment of their wishes—providing they kept to the letter of her directions. Consequently, the relationship between Roberto and Farida was doomed to failure.

For some time they sat silently, facing each other: the sturdy black woman who had a face Nefertiti could have envied, and the small, unsightly woman who forcefully stirred the steaming bowl filled with a thick, black pulp.

For the third time all the objections against the relationship between Roberto and Farida had to be told, for the third

yet, and sooner than you think!" Her eyes were no longer mournful, but looked like jet-black marbles thrown into a shell, unable to come to a standstill.

A solid hour later, when she entered the dilapidated house of Madushi, her eyes noticed the chunk of bread hanging above the doorway. "That someone could think that such a sign would withhold famine," she thought wryly. She herself felt foolish letting herself become involved with Madushi. A smell of incense and salad oil lingered in the room where Madushi practiced her shady business, her black magic, her *broea.* She was a tiny woman with a crumpled face in which a pair of venomous eyes were hidden below heavy time the pictures of the lovers, which had been brought, were glued together and torn into little pieces, and for the third time Roberto's mother wondered what was the use of that black pulp. Before she knew it she was outside again, endowed with a dirty envelope, but poorer for the payment of a large amount of money.

At home again she read and reread the instructions Madushi had given her. This time she would be extremely careful. She discovered with relief that this time she didn't have to visit her husband's grave at full moon and stammer there, spitting out "Roberida" a few times. Neither was she asked to climb the *Seru di Nokka* in the hot sun, and there grind two different kinds of cactus into the earth as fast as she could. No, this order was more easily carried out: she had to receive the two lovers and offer them *Olvidame*. The recipe for this medicine meant to kill love was encoded in virtually unreadable handwriting.

At first, Farida didn't want to hear anything about it. But, after clever Roberto played his mother's trump card, saying that she would be insulted if Farida didn't accept the invitation, she agreed to visit Roberto at home one Saturday.

When his mother offered drinks with a too-broad smile and a too-sweet voice, Roberto knew for sure that he was the victim of a shrewd play. He comforted himself with the thought that he couldn't

have escaped this trap—he hardly could have refused his mother's gesture of reconciliation. It only bothered him that he couldn't figure out what she was up to. She was positively sugary, encouraging Farida to empty her glass when, not used to alcoholic drinks, the young woman showed signs of having problems with the stiff Cuba Libre. At their parting, she embraced a loud, giggling Farida and at the same time winked at her son, which confused him even more. He was brooding so intensely about the unusual attitude of his mother that he didn't even notice how Farida had taken his arm and was pinching him now and then, laughing loudly. It was not until she kissed him provocatively on the mouth before she boarded the bus that he understood the role of the Cuba Libre in her surprising metamorphosis.

The next meeting resulted in a big argument. With a smile, he had teased her, saying that a prudish, shy Farida wasn't enough for him anymore. If she needed a Cuba Libre for a romantic tête-à-tête, he was very willing to meet her in the Delia Bar instead of the ice cream parlor. At that she had stood up and in a trembling voice declared that she was through with him, for he had deeply insulted her by insinuating that she wasn't a respectable girl, but a "bar broad." He had tried without luck to stop her, but she ran out crying. He tore up the weekly letter and sprinkled the bits of paper over her banana split, which she had barely touched. He kept his seat for a moment in order to defy the disapproving glances. Then he shook his head, clenched his fists, and left, roaring with laughter. He was sure that Farida's outburst would bring about the turn which he had awaited so long.

Madushi was taken aback: in her career she frequently had clients who returned to complain that the therapy had not worked or that the prescription had not healed them, but hardly ever had she encountered as grateful a client as this sturdy black woman who praised her so enthusiastically.

"He has been home for three Saturdays already," she cried. "Not one, not two, but three . . . three. When you die there will be a bench for you in heaven for sure." And Madushi received still another hundred guilders, a small token of huge appreciation, before Roberto's mother left, dancing.

On her way home, she bought—for an exorbitantly high price, and without bargaining—a large red snapper, some bananas to bake in slices, and corn flour for the *funchi*. She would surprise and spoil Roberto by fixing his favorite dish. She would make it as pleasant for him as possi-

ble so that he would spend all his Saturdays with her. It was true, he didn't say much and just sat staring in front of him like a ship owner who had just heard of a squall at sea, but he was there . . . thanks to Madushi.

The neighbors had noticed that she was happier, that she sang the whole day, that she played her radio too loud, and that she dismissed their problems, which once she'd listened to attentively, saying, "Look for the silver lining." Consequently, nobody bothered to come to her aid upon hearing her penetrating scream followed by her heartrending shriek. She cried the way you're allowed to cry when your mother suddenly dies, but she hadn't had a mother for a long time. When she realized that she couldn't share her grief, she stopped wailing and read and reread the note Roberto had left on the fruit bowl:

Dear Mai,
Farida and I are now sitting in the plane to Venezuela, thanks to your Cuba Libre. After our marriage, we will return to receive your maternal blessing.

Your thankful children,
Roberto and Farida

Even before the great run on Cuba as the result of Prohibition, the concept of the mixed drink was well established on the island. It had come into being as ice became easily available at the end of the nineteenth century. Besides ice, the native tropical fruits and Cuban rum were all that were required in the first *compuestos* (mixed drinks), *achampanados* (sparkling drinks), and *meneaos* (shakes).

Then after World War I, the bar business really took off. Barkeeps from all over the world—especially the United States, France, and Spain—descended on Cuba in droves. It is said that one Irishman packed up his entire establishment in New Jersey, including the mirrors, the stools, and his lighted sign, and reassembled it as Donovan's Bar in the center of Havana. The first of the bartenders to gain a wider reputation were Manteca from the Pasaje and Emilio Gonzáles—known as Maragato—from the Florida. Both of them worked in the white jacket and starched collar that soon became de rigueur. Along with the number of talented drink mixers, the number of world-famous mixed drinks grew as well. One such was the Presidente, named after Cuba's president General Menocal, whose thirst for cocktails was as well known as his lust for public monies.

In the twenties, Cuba became the cocktail capital of the world, and certain of its bars are famous as the birthplace of a specific drink. The September Morn, for example, originated in the Hotel Inglaterra, the Mary Pickford at the bar in the Hotel Sevilla. Visitors from the United States were delighted to find drinks named after their stars; they could choose between a Gloria Swanson, a Greta Garbo, a Douglas Fairbanks, or a Caruso. Other names were simply English translations of Cuban place names, such as the Isle of Pines (from Isla de Piños—also known as Isla de la Juventud), an island south of Havana where the juiciest grapefruit were grown.

In the forties and fifties, Cuba's bar and cocktail tradition continued to thrive, increasingly led by such native bartenders as José Maria Vázquez, the inventor of the Mulatta. The Mojito, a drink developed during this period, is still the most popular mixed drink in Cuba today. And the Saoco—rum and coconut milk—is a veritable Caribbean tradition.

Even under Fidel Castro, the tradition lives on. The thriving Escuela de Hotelería, in which new Cuban bartenders are trained in a classroom containing a regulation mahogany bar, was founded as early as 1962. To qualify for a Class A diploma, the student must have a minimum of 120 cocktails in his repertoire.

Cuba Libre

3 or 4 ice cubes

1¾ oz. white rum

cola to taste

¼ lime

Mix the rum and cola in a highball glass with the ice. Add the lime; stir.

Habana Libre

1 scoop crushed ice

juice of ¼ lime

2 splashes grenadine

1½ oz. white rum

¾ oz. aged white rum

Mix in highball glass. Stir well. Garnish with a wedge of lime and mint sprig.

Havana Special

1 scoop crushed ice

2 oz. pineapple juice

2 splashes maraschino

1½ oz. white rum

Mix in a shaker. Strain the mixed ingredients into a highball glass half full of crushed ice.

Bacardi Cocktail

1 scoop crushed ice

juice of ½ lime

5 splashes grenadine

1¾ oz. Bacardi

Mix in a shaker. Serve in an iced cocktail glass. (Schumann's version: in place of 5 splashes grenadine, use 2 of grenadine and 2 of sugar syrup.)

Presidente (Original Version)

6 to 8 ice cubes

¼ oz. dry vermouth

¾ oz. sweet vermouth

1½ oz. white rum

1 splash grenadine

Mix in a stirring glass. Serve in an iced cocktail glass, with a maraschino cherry.

Presidente Seco (Dry)

6 to 8 ice cubes

1 splash red curaçao

¾ oz. dry vermouth

1½ oz. white rum

Mix in a stirring glass. Serve in an iced cocktail glass, with a lemon twist.

Florida Special

1 scoop crushed ice

¾ oz. orange juice

¼ oz. maraschino

¼ oz. red curaçao (or triple sec)

1½ oz. golden rum

Mix in a shaker. Serve in an iced cocktail glass.

La Floridita Cocktail

3 or 4 ice cubes

juice of ½ lime

1 splash grenadine

¼ oz. white crème de cacao

¾ oz. sweet vermouth

1½ oz. white rum

Mix in a shaker. Serve in an iced cocktail glass.

MARY PICKFORD

1 scoop crushed ice

1½ oz. pineapple juice

1 splash grenadine

1½ oz. white rum

Mix in a shaker. Serve in an iced cocktail glass, with a maraschino cherry.

ERNEST HEMINGWAY SPECIAL

1 scoop crushed ice

juice of ½ lime

¼ oz. grapefruit juice

¼ oz. maraschino

1½ oz. white rum

Mix in a shaker. Serve in an iced cocktail glass.

MOJITO

juice of ½ lime

1 teaspoon sugar

mint leaves, to taste

crushed ice

2 oz. white rum

soda water

Preparation: Place lime juice and sugar in a highball glass; stir until sugar is dissolved. Add a few mint leaves, pressing them on the side of the glass. Fill with crushed ice; pour in the rum. Stir again. Top with soda water, and garnish with a sprig of mint.

MULATTA

1 scoop crushed ice

juice of ½ lime

¼ oz. brown crème de cacao

1¾ oz. white rum

Mix in a blender. Serve in an iced cocktail glass.

SAOCO

1 scoop crushed ice

3½ oz. coconut milk

1½ oz. white rum

Place the crushed ice in a highball glass and add coconut milk and rum. Stir thoroughly.

FLAMINGO

1 scoop crushed ice

juice of ¼ lime

a few splashes of grenadine

1 oz. pineapple juice

1½ oz. white rum

Mix in a shaker. Serve in a cocktail glass.

SEPTEMBER MORN

1 scoop crushed ice

juice of ¼ lime

a few splashes of grenadine

1 teaspoon sugar

1 egg white

1¾ oz. white rum

Mix in a shaker. Serve in an iced cocktail glass.

BOINA ROJA

Red Beret

1 scoop crushed ice

juice of ½ lime

2 splashes grenadine

¾ oz. white rum

1½ oz. aged white rum

Mix in a highball glass; garnish with a sprig of mint and a maraschino cherry.

PERIODISTA

Journalist

1 scoop crushed ice

juice of ½ lime

1 teaspoon sugar

2 splashes apricot brandy

2 splashes triple sec

1½ oz. white rum

Mix in a shaker. Serve in a cocktail glass, with a lime twist.

CENTENARIO

1 scoop crushed ice

juice of 1 lime

¼ oz. grenadine

¼ oz. Tia Maria

¼ oz. triple sec

¾ oz. aged white rum

1½ oz. golden rum

Mix well in a highball glass. Garnish with a mint sprig.

TRICONTINENTAL

crushed ice

¼ oz. grenadine

¼ oz. brown crème de cacao

2 oz. golden rum

Fill a champagne flute with crushed ice. Carefully add the ingredients in the order given so that they sit one on top of the other.

ISLE OF PINES

Isla de Pinos

3 or 4 ice cubes

2 oz. grapefruit juice

1½ oz. white rum

Mix in a highball glass.

On his return to Haiti, my grandfather found everything changed. A hurricane had devastated the island and destroyed most of the harvest. Hungry peasants from the interior had plundered Port-au-Prince and ransacked the Presidential Palace. It had cost the army under the aged general Pierre Nord Alexis heavy losses to drive them out of the capital. My grandfather's house on the Chemin des Dalles had not been spared. Books and furniture had been stolen or used for firewood; only the Bechstein piano, like a rock in a tempest, had weathered the popular fury. Herr Stecher, my grandfather's partner, along with the deposed president's entourage, had fled to Jamaica and applied for political asylum. Before leaving, he had sold the pharmacy with all its furnishings and stock, and deposited the proceeds in his bank.

Another man might have been discouraged by two such cruel blows. My grandfather, however, who always saw the bright side of the most hopeless situations, decided to indulge a long-cherished wish, which his wife's delicate health had hitherto caused him to shelve. Along with Dr. Dupuis, who was working on an archaeological study of the culture of the Carib Indians who had inhabited Haiti before the conquest, he set out on a botanical foray into the interior. For safety's sake they attached themselves to a punitive expedition led by General Nord Alexis against the rebellious peasants, who had withdrawn to the mountains after pillaging the capital. The two friends rode at the head of the troops, side by side with the aged general, who had been fighting these rebels for a generation with varied success and knew the rugged interior like the back of his hand. . . .

The general rode a Spanish stallion, while my grandfather and Dr. Dupuis shared the stout back of a mule. They also had a number of pack asses with them, on which they had loaded their scientific equipment, spades, specimen containers, and a barrel of rum, which served to quench their thirst, disinfect wounds, and preserve specimens. My grandfather was planning to use the barrel on the way back to house a cayman that Professor Grzimek had ordered for the Frankfurt Zoo. Once the soldiers had found out what was in the barrel, my grandfather had to keep an eye open all night and occasionally fire his Krupp repeating rifle into the air as a warning to would-be marauders. Now and

then the doctor relieved him of his sentry duty. The small advance guard rode along the dry bed of the Artibonite River, which was ordinarily in full flood at that time of year. What had once been a luxuriant green plain, covered with cane fields and bamboo groves, had become a desert shimmering in the heat. The dust stuck to the lips of the thirsty men and gritted between their teeth.

"This time," said the general, "we'll teach the rebels a lesson they'll never forget, because they won't have time to." Raising his binoculars to his eyes, he searched the surrounding hilltops. Two eagles were circling overhead; in their bird's-eye view the marching army looked like a snake crawling through the desert. "I admit, we haven't got the most modern equipment," the general went on, looking enviously at my grandfather's Krupp repeating rifle, "but when it comes to fighting spirit, my grenadiers are the equal of any modern army, not to mention those illiterate peasants, who know nothing of military strategy and tactics."

The general had not finished speaking when my grandfather fired two shots. The eagles fell dead at his feet, but then, as though my grandfather's shots had given the enemy entrenched behind the riverbank the signal to attack, rifle fire was heard from all directions. The soldiers threw down their guns and fled with wild screams, while the general, whose face

had turned ashen, took cover behind a clump of cactuses and ordered his artillerymen to load the mortar. No sooner had the mortar been put into position than a dispatch rider, whose horse had bolted during the volley of rifle fire, came running up to the general and informed him that it had all been a false alarm: because of the extreme heat my grandfather's shots had sparked off a chain reaction in a sandbox tree, whose seed capsules had exploded with a sound like rifle fire.

"I'm afraid I'm too old for soldiering," said the general, coming out from his clump of cactuses and wiping the sweat from his forehead. "Seventy years are no joke," he said. "My senses would never have tricked me like that in my younger days. Let's have a swig of your rum, my dear Louis. If anything should happen to me on this campaign, I want you and Dr. Dupuis to take command."

When my grandfather tried to give the general his drink, he discovered to his dismay that a bullet fired by mistake during the momentary panic had pierced the rum barrel. Its precious contents were trickling irretrievably away. While he was trying vainly to plug the hole, the general, intoxicated by the rum fumes, fell to the ground in a faint. The doctor was bending over to feel the general's pulse when a deafening thunderclap was heard, followed by an underground rumbling as of distant gunfire. Awakened by the noise, the general opened his eyes. Was it an earthquake? Or had the hostile Dominican Republic equipped the rebels with modern artillery? The general had no time to answer these questions, for in that moment a flash flood came roaring over the dry riverbed. The foaming waves drove before them an avalanche of rock and underbrush, uprooted trees and peasant huts, occupants and all. In a matter of seconds the surrounding plain became a watery waste, and in its muddy waves the entire Eighth Field Army perished, leaving not the slightest trace in history. Only an occasional officer's sword or soldier's cookpot that had been caught in the prickly arms of a cactus or the thorny branches of a sandbox tree emerged here and there from the water. A rifle butt hit my grandfather on the head, and the world went black before his eyes.

In his dream, he was wandering through a jungle dimly lit by glowworms. Deep within it, on a bed of water lilies, a naked water nymph was waiting for him. Her hair was powdered with gold dust, and she was combing it with a silver comb. Her eyes were as deep and dark as the black water into which she drew him in an embrace of overpowering sweetness, from which he would never have awakened if his shirt collar hadn't got caught on a forked branch and held him above water.

When he opened his eyes, what he was holding in his arms was not a naked water nymph but the empty rum barrel, which was still giving off heady alcohol fumes. His rear end was aflame. The flood had thrown him, along with the barrel he was clutching, into the open arms of a cactus, whose prickly embrace had saved his life. Clogged with mud and vegetation, his repeating rifle was hanging from his shoulder. The painful lump on his forehead was where the stock had hit him. Otherwise, apart from the prickles in his behind, which he was acutely aware of every time he moved, he was unhurt. The flood had receded as quickly as it had come, and only a few mud puddles bore witness to the cataclysm that had engulfed a whole army. The entire plain, as far as the eye could see, was covered with mud. Already ravens and vultures had made themselves at home on the swollen bellies of dead horses and asses, which emerged from the mud like islands. Two steps away, he distinguished the barrel of the mortar, half buried in the muck; its broken wheels spun with a rasping sound when the wind caught the spokes, and at a little distance, framed by neatly aligned bayonets sticking out of the mud, the general's cap floated like a boat on a puddle lashed by falling rain. Using his repeating rifle as a pole, my grandfather fished the cap out of the water, with the intention of giving it as a memento to the general's widow on his return to the capital. Just then he heard a terrified neighing and saw, close above

him, in the branches of a sandbox tree, the spotted belly of a mule, lashing out with its hind legs at a cayman that had got hold of its tail and was trying to pull it into the water. On the mule's back sat the trembling doctor, who welcomed my grandfather as a savior. With a shot from his repeating rifle, which disgorged more mud and vegetation than lead, he drove the rapacious monster away, and a moment later, with the help of a lasso, he freed the doctor from his awkward situation.

The friends' first thought, after congratulating each other on their miraculous rescue, was for the rum barrel, which was not quite empty; a little rum, they thought, would come in handy on the return journey. After plugging the bullet hole with the seed pod of a sandbox tree and fishing their luggage out of various ponds, they resumed their journey. They could not return directly to the capital, for the flood had made the roads impassable, nor did it seem advisable: they feared that, being

the sole survivors, they would be held responsible for the destruction of the Eighth Army. After saddling their mule, they therefore took a narrow path leading to the mountains, where their mount soon had solid ground under its hoofs. The fruitful island lay stretched out at their feet under a sky as pure as when Columbus first landed on this coast. Only here and there could smoke be seen rising, but from the distance it was hard to tell whether a wood was being cleared, stubble burned, or a peaceful village razed. The sun had passed the zenith and was inclining toward the western horizon. The friends unsaddled their mule and fastened their hammocks to the wide-spreading branches of a monkey-bread tree, the fruit of which supplied them with a simple but tasty supper. With a swig from the rum barrel they bade the parting day good night, wrapped themselves in their mosquito netting, and slept soundly until morning.

My grandfather was up and about before sunrise. With butterfly net and specimen container, he explored the countryside while the doctor lay snoring in his hammock. Myriad dew drops glittered on the emerald-green grass, and a chorus of mountain parrots was greeting the rising sun. My grandfather was disentangling an orchid from a hanging liana when he glimpsed nearby a shimmering gold butterfly, reeling, drunk with love, from flower to flower. Eager to capture this rare specimen of *Botys reginalis* of the Pyralididae family for his collection, my grandfather followed the butterfly, which seemed to hover motionless, its wings fluttering, but evaded him every time he prepared to throw his net over it, so luring him deeper and deeper into the forest. When he finally noticed that the elusive butterfly had led him astray, it was too late. Throwing his butterfly net away, he sank exhausted to the forest floor.

He heard a splashing of water from not far away and, shifting an overhanging branch, he caught sight of a waterfall. In its spray the slanting beams of the sun painted concentric rainbows, whose iridescent light made him think of a stained-glass window in a Gothic cathedral. Under the arching rainbow sat a nude woman running a silver comb through her flowing hair. My grandfather's first impulse was to go away discreetly, but the young woman had already seen him. With a silent glance she bade him follow her. Behind the curtain of spray lay the entrance to a cave faintly lit by glowworms, which, as my grandfather recognized on closer scrutiny, were butterflies of the Pyralididae family, unloading the gold dust they had gathered in the mountains. The good fairy—for that's what she was—took my grandfather by the hand and led him through secret passages with clusters of bats clinging to their walls, to an underground treasure room, where the gold was smelted in a volcanic smithy and wrought into ornaments, goblets and statues that reminded my grandfather of Aztec idols: infants and old men, hunchbacks and parturient women, who instead of human faces had the beaks of parrots, the claws and fangs of caymans and jaguars.

The fairy told my grandfather he had nothing to fear. "The common people," she said, "call me Maman Zimbie, because I make my home in springs and ponds. They think if anyone looks me in the eye I'll pull them into the water. But that's superstitious nonsense. My real name is Anacoana, and I'm the queen of the Taino Indians. . . . I've chosen you to keep my race from dying out."

With these words, she drew him down on her bed of water lilies and lianas, and he didn't leave it for seven years. . . .

The seven years passed like a dream. My grandfather would gladly have stayed on in Anacoana's cave, where he wanted for nothing, but after the birth of her seven sons she had no further use for him and sent him home, making him swear not to breathe a word about what he had seen and heard in her underground realm. When he asked for some of her gold as a parting gift, she explained that she had already made him a priceless present: the pod with which he had plugged the leak in his barrel was more precious than gold; it was not the pod of a sandbox tree, but a cola nut, the miraculous fruit that had enabled the priests of the Taino Indians to talk with the gods. My grandfather, she said, had only to grate a bit of the nut and mix the resulting powder with water and rum. He was a made man, provided he reveal the secret of this magic potion to no one.

My grandfather was quick to act on her advice. He had no sooner crossed the waterfall and returned to their campsite, where the doctor still lay snoring in his hammock—it seems that not seven years but only seven minutes had passed—than he put the good fairy's recipe to the test. Lying on his back beside the rum barrel, he pulled the stopper and let the dark-brown liquid, which had fermented overnight, run out into his mouth. The result was staggering: after the very first swallow he felt blissfully refreshed and euphoric, at once drunk and sober. He would gladly have drained the whole barrel in one draft. Instead, however, he decided to strike while the iron was hot and exploit his discovery without delay. Quietly, so as not to wake the doctor, with whom he would otherwise have had to share the profits, he stood up, saddled the mule, and started rolling the barrel down the mountain. He was in such a hurry that the mule could hardly keep up with him.

When he got to Port-au-Prince, the scene left him speechless with amazement. The streets sparkled in the sunlight as if there had never been a flood; the houses were decked with flags and streamers. The whole population was on the streets. . . . The President of the Republic, wearing his tricolored sash of office, came to meet my grandfather with open arms and bade him a fraternal welcome. Then at last my grandfather realized what had happened: the good fairy's prophecy had come true sooner than he could have hoped, for the new president was none other than the aged general. The flood, which had engulfed his whole army, had carried him directly to the capital and the summit of power. . . . My grandfather handed the general his mislaid cap, which is still on display at the Historical Museum of Port-au-Prince, and was rewarded with an appropriate decoration. In return for his observance of strict silence about the recent campaign, the President appointed him purveyor extraordinary of pharmaceuticals to the army and gave him an unrestricted license to manufacture a cooling beverage that was later, under the trademark Coca-Cola, to conquer the world.

Every classical cocktail has three chief components: the base, a modifier or aromatizer, and a coloring agent or special flavoring. In the classic rum drinks, for example, the base is rum, the modifier an Italian or French vermouth, a special fruit juice, or sugar. The third component might well be a fruit syrup such as grenadine, a brandy, or a fruit liqueur such as apricot brandy or Cointreau. Whatever the special flavoring, it should never overpower the flavor of the basic rum. A cocktail based on rum should always taste like rum.

Many classic rum cocktails were fashioned after other well-known drinks. The Pedro Collins or Rum Collins is simply a variation on the older John Collins and Tom Collins, both of which were invented by the bartender at Limmer's Hotel in London at the beginning of the nineteenth century. His name was John Collins, and the cocktail he created on a base of Geneva gin bears his name. His subsequent drink based on Old Tom gin became a Tom Collins.

Rum can equally well replace the base alcohol in a Manhattan, an Old Fashioned, a Gimlet, a Fizz, or a Highball.

Common modifiers are Italian or French vermouths. These are wines flavored with the extracts of as many as fifty aromatic herbs, including wormwood. Most vermouths have an alcohol content of roughly 16 percent, dry vermouths at least 18 percent.

A great number of different liqueurs and brandies are employed as flavorings. Rum blends especially well with such fruit brandies as Cointreau (flavored with the peel of bitter oranges), the famous apple brandy calvados, or apricot brandy. Another liqueur made of bitter oranges is Creole Clement, which is produced by the rum distiller Clement from Martinique. Southern Comfort, a liqueur based on bourbon whiskey but with a distinct aroma of peaches, is another staple. In addition to peaches, oranges and various herbs are used in making Southern Comfort.

Then there are the distinctly tropical liqueurs. Tia Maria is one of these. It is made in Jamaica from tropical herbs, vanilla, sugarcane sap, and Blue Mountain coffee beans. Curaçao is another. Curaçao is a generic name for any liqueur distilled from the peel of the curaçao fruit—or Seville orange—which was originally grown only on the Dutch island of the same name. Other tropical products are Kahlúa, a Mexican coffee liqueur, and Eau de Créole, a West Indian one made from the blossoms of the mammee tree.

Any liqueur whose name begins with "crème de . . ." is bound to be especially sweet.

The most important crème liqueurs for bar use are:

Crème de Cacao (white and brown)
Crème de Menthe (white and green)
Crème de Bananes
Crème de Vanille (Galliano)
Crème de Cassis

All of these liqueurs must be used with great discretion. Too much in a cocktail tends to destroy the aroma of the base alcohol, making the drink unenjoyable.

BLACK DEVIL

Rum Martini

6 to 8 ice cubes

¼ oz. dry vermouth

1¾ oz. white rum

Mix in a stirring glass. Strain into an iced martini glass or an iced small cocktail glass. Garnish with a black olive.

RUM OLD FASHIONED

1 cube of sugar, laced with 2 to 3 splashes Angostura

3 to 4 ice cubes

1¾ oz. white rum

ice water or soda water

Mix in an old fashioned glass. Add a maraschino cherry and wedges of lemon and orange. Top with ice water or soda water.

CUBAN MANHATTAN (SWEET)

6 to 8 ice cubes

1 splash Angostura

¾ oz. sweet vermouth

1½ oz. white rum

Mix in a stirring glass. Strain into an iced cocktail glass and serve with a maraschino cherry.

CUBAN MANHATTAN (DRY)

Mix as the sweet Cuban Manhattan, using ¾ oz. dry vermouth in place of the sweet vermouth, and serve with a lemon twist.

CUBAN MANHATTAN (MEDIUM)

6 to 8 ice cubes

¼ oz. dry vermouth

¼ oz. sweet vermouth

1½ oz. white rum

Mix as the sweet Cuban Manhattan. In the Cuban Manhattan, it is perfectly acceptable to substitute equal portions of rum and vermouth: 1 oz. dry or sweet vermouth to 1 oz. white rum.

Rum Sour

3 or 4 ice cubes

¾ oz. lemon juice

¾ oz. sugar syrup or 2 teaspoons sugar

1½ oz. white rum

¼ oz. golden rum

Mix in a shaker. Serve in a whiskey sour glass, with a maraschino cherry.

Rum Stinger

3 or 4 ice cubes, or crushed ice

¾ oz. white crème de menthe

1½ oz. white rum

Combine the ingredients and stir in the old fashioned glass the drink is to be served in.
(As an alternative, use equal 1-oz. measures of crème de menthe and rum.)

Rum Gimlet

1 small scoop crushed ice

1 oz. Rose's Lime Juice

1¾ oz. white rum

Mix in a stirring glass. Strain into an iced cocktail glass. Add a twist of lime.

(Schumann's version: mix in a shaker. In order to offset the sweetness of the Rose's Lime Juice, I add a little fresh lime or lemon juice. Too much, however, turns the gimlet into a sour.)

Rum Sazerac

3 or 4 ice cubes

1 cube of sugar, laced with 2 splashes Angostura

2 splashes Pernod

2 oz. white rum

ice water

Mix directly in an old fashioned glass. Top with water, stir, and add a twist of lemon.

RUM ALEXANDER

3 or 4 ice cubes

1 oz. cream

¾ oz. brown crème de cacao

1½ oz. white rum

nutmeg

Mix in a shaker. Strain into a cocktail glass. Top with a little grated nutmeg.

CRÉOLE

3 or 4 ice cubes

2 splashes lemon juice

3½ oz. beef bouillon

1¾ oz. white rum

pepper, salt, Tabasco, Worcestershire sauce, to taste

Mix first four ingredients in a highball glass. Flavor to taste and stir.

PEDRO COLLINS

Rum Collins

3 or 4 ice cubes

1 oz. lemon or lime juice

½ oz. sugar syrup

1¾ oz. white rum

soda water

Mix in a highball glass. Stir well and fill with soda water. Garnish with a maraschino cherry and lemon wedge.

BETWEEN THE SHEETS

3 or 4 ice cubes

¾ oz. lemon juice

¾ oz. triple sec

¾ oz. brandy

¾ oz. white rum

Mix in a shaker. Serve in an iced cocktail glass.

RUM FIZZ

Use the same ingredients as in the Pedro Collins, but mix in a shaker and top with soda water.

Apricot Lady

1 scoop crushed ice

juice of ½ lime

1 egg white

¾ oz. apricot brandy

1½ oz. white rum

Mix in a shaker. Serve in an iced cocktail glass.

Columbus Cocktail

1 scoop crushed ice

juice of ½ lime

¾ oz. apricot brandy

1½ oz. golden rum

Mix in a shaker. Serve in an iced cocktail glass.

Havana Sidecar

3 or 4 ice cubes, or crushed ice

¾ oz. lemon juice

¾ oz. triple sec

1½ oz. golden rum

Mix in a shaker. Serve in an iced cocktail glass.

Acapulco

3 or 4 ice cubes, or crushed ice

juice of ½ lime

1 teaspoon sugar or 2 splashes sugar syrup

1 egg white

¼ oz. triple sec

1¾ oz. white rum

Mix in a shaker. Serve in an iced cocktail glass.

FIESTA COCKTAIL

1 scoop crushed ice

1 splash lime juice

1 splash grenadine

¾ oz. Noilly Prat

¾ oz. calvados

¾ oz. white rum

Mix in a shaker or stirring glass. Serve in an iced cocktail glass.

QUAKER'S COCKTAIL

1 scoop crushed ice

juice of ½ lime

2 splashes raspberry syrup

¾ oz. brandy

¾ oz. white rum

Mix in a shaker. Serve in an iced cocktail glass.

SIR WALTER COCKTAIL

1 scoop crushed ice

juice of ½ lime

1 splash grenadine

¼ oz. triple sec

¾ oz. brandy

1 oz. golden rum

Mix in a shaker. Serve in an iced cocktail glass.

BLACK WIDOW

3 or 4 ice cubes

juice of ½ lime

1 splash sugar syrup

½ oz. Southern Comfort

1 oz. golden rum

Mix in a shaker. Serve in an iced cocktail glass.

Liberty Cocktail

1 scoop crushed ice

juice of ½ lime

1 teaspoon sugar

¾ oz. applejack

1½ oz. white rum

Mix in a shaker. Serve in an iced cocktail glass.

Rum Screwdriver

3 or 4 ice cubes

3½ oz. orange juice

1¾ oz. white rum

Mix in a highball glass.
(You can substitute brown for white rum.)

Rum Highball

3 or 4 ice cubes

1¾ oz. white (or brown) rum

ginger ale, soda water, or Seven Up, to taste

Mix in a highball glass. Garnish with a spiral of lemon zest.

Iced Tea

crushed ice

¾ oz. orange juice

¾ oz. triple sec

¾ oz. brandy

¾ oz. white rum

¾ oz. brown rum

juice of ½ lime

cola to taste

Place the crushed ice in a tall drink glass and add the first five ingredients. Stir well. Add the lime and top with cola.

The long long day was not yet over: midnight was an hour or an age away. I took my car and drove along the edge of the sea, the road pitted with holes. There were very few people about; perhaps they had not realized the curfew was raised or they feared a trap. On my right hand were a line of wooden huts in little fenced saucers of earth where a few palm-trees grew and slithers of water gleamed between, like scrap-iron on a dump. An occasional candle burned over a little group bowed above their rum like mourners over a coffin. Sometimes there were furtive sounds of music. An old man danced in the middle of the road—I had to brake my car to a standstill. He came and giggled at me through the glass—at least there was one man in Port-au-Prince that night who was not afraid. I couldn't make out the meaning of his *patois* and I drove on. It was two years or more since I had been to Mère Catherine's, but tonight I needed her services. My impotence lay in my body like a curse which it needed a witch to raise. I thought of the girl on East 56th Street, and when reluctantly I thought of Martha I whipped up my anger. If she had made love to me when I had wanted her, this would not be happening.

Just before Mère Catherine's the road branched—the tarmac, if you could call it tarmac, came to an abrupt end (money had run out or someone hadn't received his cut). To the left was the main southern highway, almost impassable except by jeep. I was surprised to find a road-block there, for no one expected invasion from the south. I stood, while they searched me more carefully than usual, under a great placard which announced "U.S.A.-Haitian Joint Five Year Plan. Great Southern Highway," but the Americans had left and nothing remained of all the five-year plan but the notice-board, over the stagnant pools, the channels in the road, the rocks, and the carcass of a dredger which nobody had bothered to rescue from the mud.

After they let me go I took the right fork and arrived at Mère Catherine's compound. All was so quiet I wondered whether it was worth my while to leave the car. A long low hut like a stable divided into stalls were the quarters here for love. I could see a light burning in the main building where Mère Catherine received her guests and served them drinks, but there was no sound of music and dancing. For a moment fidelity became a temptation and I wanted to drive away. But I had carried my malady too far along the rough road to be put off now, and I moved cautiously across the dark compound towards the light, hating myself all the way. I had foolishly turned the car against the wall of the hut, so that I was in darkness, and almost at once I stumbled against a jeep, standing lightless; a man slept at the wheel. Again I nearly turned and went, for there were few jeeps in Port-au-Prince

which were not owned by the Tontons Macoute, and if the Tontons Macoute were making a night of it with Mère Catherine's girls, there would be no room for outside custom.

But I was obstinate in my self-hatred, and I went on. Mère Catherine heard me stumbling and came to meet me on the threshold, holding up an oil-lamp. She had the face of a kind nanny in a film of the deep South, and a tiny delicate body which must once have been beautiful. Her face didn't belie her nature, for she was the kindest woman I knew in Port-au-Prince. She pretended that her girls came from good families, that she was only helping them to earn a little pin-money, and you could almost believe her, for she had taught them perfect manners in public. Till they reached the stalls her customers too had to behave with decorum, and to watch the couples dance you would almost have believed it to be an end-of-term celebration at a convent-school. On one occasion three years before I had seen her go in to rescue a girl from some brutality. I was drinking a glass of rum and I heard a scream from what we called the stable, but before I could decide what to do Mère Catherine had taken a hatchet from the kitchen and sailed out like the little *Revenge* prepared to take on a fleet. Her opponent was armed with a knife, he was twice her size, and he was drunk with rum. (He must have had a flask in his hip-

pocket, for Mère Catherine would never have allowed him to go outside with a girl in that condition.) He turned and fled at her approach, and later when I left, I saw her through the window of the kitchen, with the girl upon her knee, crooning to her as though she were a child, in a *patois* which I couldn't understand, and the girl slept against the little bony shoulder.

Mère Catherine whispered a warning to me, "The Tontons are here."

"All the girls taken?"

"No, but the girl you like is busy."

I hadn't been here for two years, but she remembered, and what was even more remarkable the girl was with her still— she would be close on eighteen by now. I hadn't expected to find her, and yet I was disappointed. In age one prefers old friends, even in a *bordel*.

"Are they in a dangerous mood?" I asked her.

"I don't think so. They are looking after someone important. He's out with Tin Tin now."

I nearly went away, but my grudge against Martha worked like an infection.

"I'll come in," I said. "I'm thirsty. Give me a rum and Coke."

"There's no more Coke." I had forgotten that American aid was over.

"Rum and soda then."

"I have a few bottles of Seven-up left."

"All right. Seven-up."

At the door of the *salle* a Tonton Macoute was asleep on a chair; his sun-glasses had fallen into his lap and he looked quite harmless. The flies of his grey flannel trousers gaped from a lost button. Inside there was complete silence. Through the open door I saw a group of four girls dressed in white muslin with balloon-skirts. They were sucking orangeade through straws, not speaking. One of them took her empty glass and moved away, walking beautifully, the muslin swaying, like a little bronze by Degas.

"No customers at all?"

"They all left when the Tontons Macoute came."

I went in, and there at a table by the wall with his eyes fixed on me as though I had never once escaped from them was the Tonton Macoute I had seen in the police-station, who had smashed the windows of the hearse to get out the coffin of the *ancien ministre*. His soft hat lay on a chair, and he wore a striped bow-tie. I bowed to him and started towards another table. I was scared of him, and I wondered whom it could be—more important than this arrogant officer—that Tin Tin was consoling now. I hoped for her sake he was not a worse man as well.

The officer said, "I seem to see you everywhere."

"I try to be inconspicuous."

"What do you want here tonight?"

"A rum and Seven-up."

He said to Mère Catherine, who was bringing in my drink upon a tray, "You said you had no Seven-up left." I noticed that there was an empty soda-water bottle on the tray beside my glass. The Tonton Macoute took my drink and tasted it. "Seven-up it is. You can bring this man a rum and soda. We need all the Seven-up you have left for my friend when he returns."

"It's so dark in the bar. The bottles must have got mixed."

"You must learn to distinguish between your important customers and," he hesitated and decided to be reasonably polite, "the less important. You can sit down," he said to me.

I turned away.

"You can sit down here. Sit down."

I obeyed. He said, "You were stopped at the cross-roads and searched?"

"Yes."

"And at the door here? You were stopped at the door?"

"By Mère Catherine, yes."

"By one of my men?"

"He was asleep."

"Asleep?"

"Yes."

I had no hesitation in telling tales. Let the Tontons Macoute destroy themselves. I was surprised when he said nothing and made no move towards the door. He only stared blankly through me with his black opaque lenses. He had decided something, but he would not let me know his

decision. Mère Catherine brought me in my drink. I tasted it. The rum was still mixed with Seven-up. She was a brave woman.

I said, "You seem to be taking a lot of precautions tonight."

"I am in charge of a very important foreigner. I have to take precautions for his security. He asked to come here."

"Is he safe with little Tin Tin? Or do you keep a guard in the bedroom, captain? Or is it commandant?"

"My name is Captain Concasseur. You have a sense of humour. I appreciate humour. I am in favour of jokes. They have political value. Jokes are a release for the cowardly and the impotent."

"You said an important foreigner, captain? This morning I had the impression that you didn't like foreigners."

"My personal view of every white man is very low. I admit I am offended by the colour, which reminds me of turd. But we accept some of you—if you are useful to the State."

"You mean to the Doctor?"

With a very small inflexion of irony he quoted, "*Je suis le drapeau Haïtien, Uni et Indivisible.*" He took a drink of rum. "Of course some white men are more tolerable than others. At least the French have a common culture with us. I admire the General. The President has written to him offering to join *la Communauté de l'Europe.*"

"Has he received a reply?"

"These things take time. There are conditions which we have to discuss. We understand diplomacy. We don't blunder like the Americans—and the British."

I was haunted by the name Concasseur. Somewhere I had heard it before. The first syllable suited him well, and perhaps the whole name, with its suggestion of destructive power, had been adopted like that of Stalin or Hitler.

"Haiti belongs by right to any Third Force," Captain Concasseur said. "We are the true bastion against the Communists. No Castro can succeed here. We have a loyal peasantry."

"Or a terrified one." I took a long drink of rum; drink helped to make his pretensions more supportable. "Your important visitor is taking his time."

"He told me he had been away from women for a long time." He barked at

Mère Catherine, "I want service. Service," and stamped the floor. "Why is no one dancing?"

"A bastion of the free world," I said.

The four girls rose from their table, and one put on the gramophone. They began to dance together in a graceful slow old-fashioned style. Their balloon skirts swung like silver censers and showed their slender legs the colour of young deer; they smiled gently at each other and held one another a little apart. They were beautiful and undifferentiated, like birds of the same plumage. It was impossible to believe they were for sale. Like everyone else.

"Of course the free world pays better," I said, "and in dollars."

Captain Concasseur saw where I was looking; he missed nothing through those black glasses. He said, "I will treat you to a woman. That small girl there, with a flower in her hair, Louise. She doesn't look at us. She is shy because she thinks I might be jealous. Jealous of a *putain*! What absurdity! She will serve you very well if I give her the word."

"I don't want a woman." I could see through his apparent generosity. One flings a *putain* to a white man as one flings a bone to a dog.

"Then why are you here?"

He had a right to ask the question. I could only say, "I've changed my mind," as I watched the girls revolve, worthy of a better setting than the wooden shed, the rum-bar, and the old advertisements for Coca-Cola.

71

The new Minister of Tourism is playing backgammon with the hotel's proprietess. What else should he be doing? In the year that has seen the fall of Baby Doc, Haiti has no tourists to look after.

Sixteen years ago I could hardly believe in the actual existence of the hotel on whose veranda I again now find myself. "With its towers and balconies and wooden fretwork decorations it had the air at night of a Charles Addams house in a number of the *New Yorker*. You expected a witch to open the door to you or a maniac butler, with a bat dangling from the chandelier behind him. But in the sunlight, or when the lights went on among the palms, it seemed fragile and period and pretty and absurd, an illustration from a book of fairy tales." In his novel *The Comedians*, Graham Greene changed only a single detail in his description of this magical, honey-colored wooden pleasure palace lying in its untended gardens above the bay of Port-au-Prince: his name for it is Hotel Trianon. Yet he has Mr. Brown, its owner and the narrator of the story, confess that "no name could have been less suitable." More appropriately, even for a novel, the actual name above the entry reads: Grand Hotel Oloffson. (It is said that a Norwegian captain ran his ship aground in Port-au-Prince sometime back in the twenties.)

If you have read Greene's *Comedians*, you are immediately at home here. On your arrival you give a nod to the pictures of cock fights and the voodoo images that line the creaking stairway, renderings by pupils and children of the famous naive painters Hippolyte and Obin. And you are drawn up short on seeing the door with a small sign reading "Sir John Gielgud Suite." In truth (by which I mean the novel) this special room is dedicated to the memory of the no less legendary actor John Barrymore.

And what happened on this balcony? Oh, right: it was here, you remember, that Mr. Smith stood—Mr. Smith from Wisconsin, the presidential candidate of the Vegetarian Party of America in the election of 1948 ("the man defeated by Truman")—and just missed discovering the corpse of Dr. Philipot, the discredited Minister of Welfare in the Duvalier cabinet, who had slashed his throat with a steak knife in the hotel's empty swimming pool.

The presidential candidate of the Vegetarian Party of America is no longer here, unfortunately. And in Mr. A. A. Seitz, the deceased owner of the Oloffson, you would not have recognized our old friend Brown, whom Greene cast as the heir to the Trianon and the central figure in *The Comedians'* cast of characters. But perhaps the actual proprietor resembled one of the other men in the novel? For the way Mr. Seitz smoked his huge cigars was too splendid, too convincing and authentic; it was ready-made for fiction. On this point, reality reached into the heart of the novel and resurrected the proprietor in Señor Pineda, the South American ambassador ("Nationality: human being; distinguishing feature: horns"). It was this gentleman's wife, Martha, who spent uncomfortable nights of passion with the narrator Brown in the diplomatic Peugeot down by the harbor, where a cast iron Columbus gazes out at the Caribbean Sea.

None of his characters, Greene carefully notes in his foreword to the novel, had ever existed. Resemblances were purely coincidental. "A physical trait taken here, a habit of speech, an anecdote—they are boiled up in the kitchen of the unconscious and emerge unrecognizable even to the cook in most cases." Yet Graham Greene's candid introduction is not to be taken seriously; it is already part of the story.

Petit Pierre, for example, the graceful, dandified mulatto with the bamboo cane (in Creole, *cocómacaque*) and the "constant euphoric expression that was totally unjustified," suddenly turned up in person during my first visit sixteen years ago. From the pages of the novel he stepped straight out onto the veranda of the Oloffson to immortalize me in the gossip column of his newspaper. It is amazing how precise metaphorical language can be: "He had the quick movements of a monkey, and he seemed to swing from wall to wall on ropes of laughter." The character known in the novel as Petit Pierre is actually Aubelin Jolicoeur (Greene could not have invented a better name himself). In 1970 he was still writing the society column for Haiti's largest newspaper, *Le Nouvelliste*, and paying for his drinks on the veranda of the Oloffson "only with his pen." Petit Pierre is proof that Greene "lifted" not only specific traits he observed while in Haiti, but whole people, and did so with photographic exactitude. He also suggests how for its part the novel began to have an influence on Haiti, the portrait affecting the sitter.

Graham Greene had met the young Aubelin Jolicoeur in 1954, during the giddy heyday of the general and playboy Paul Magloire. It was a time when New York celebrities were coming to Haiti and it was not uncommon to find yourself sipping rum punch with the likes of Noël Coward, Paulette Goddard, or Irving Berlin at the bar in the Oloffson. Truman Capote, then still a delicate and strikingly photogenic young writer, introduced his friend Jolicoeur to the world-famous novelist who had just "done" Indochina in *The Quiet American*. Neither of them suspected that Haiti would also inspire a novel, or that Jolicoeur would figure as one of its more colorful characters. In 1954, Haiti was not yet the perfect setting for a Greene novel; it lacked one essential element, the background of political terror. Thanks to the dictator Duvalier, this was supplied a mere three years later.

In his foreword, Greene assures us that

he has not painted the governing tactics of Dr. Duvalier in more sinister colors for dramatic effect. It would be, he writes, "impossible to deepen that night." But perhaps it was the flirtation with fear that made Haiti so interesting to knowledge-able jet-setters during those years? We do not know whether Papa Doc Duvalier, Baby Doc, or the ubiquitous *tontons macoute* ever laid their hands on the white folks during their twenty-nine-year reign; their American protectors—from Eisenhower to Reagan—would surely not have looked kindly on such a misstep. The only danger to whites during the three decades these two "presidents for life" were in power was that any revolt against their regime could degenerate into a general bloodbath in which no one was safe, not even white tourists.

But at that time such an uprising was only a remote possibility. In the lee of class conflict between the ruling mulatto minority and the black majority, one that Duvalier shrewdly manipulated in the most racist terms, the tiny white community lived very well indeed. Arabs and Jews dominated commerce, while Americans, Scandinavians, and Germans made vast sums of money and lived like feudal lords. For them, Haiti was—and still is—simply a fascinating backdrop for their acquisitive and glittering lives. Tourists, reporters—and the writer Graham Greene—could hardly have avoided the same observation. Sincerely moved by the Haitian reality, but frankly uninvolved and safely detached, they perceived themselves as actors on some exotic stage, protagonists in a fantastic tale, flesh-and-blood fictional characters.

Brenda Slemenson, who sits across from me now on the veranda in her flowered robe and pink slippers, and has just ordered me another rum punch, has seen her share of both terror and misery. Still, she announces, "I'll give you California, I'll give you Paris and London for Port-au-Prince." When a German businessman said the same thing to me I was not surprised. The villa in Pétionville, the Buick Riviera, the armed chauffeur, the pretty coffee-colored wife—all of this made his assertion perfectly understandable. But the blonde Brenda doesn't own any sisal plantations, has no chauffeured limousines or bodyguards. Why then, at forty-five, blonde, divorced, and with a good figure and sense of humor, does she keep sitting on the veranda of the Oloffson? The taciturn black poet, whose hand she clutches like the arm of a chair, is not the answer, for tomorrow Brenda will show up in the dining room, with her Mona Lisa smile and her eyes dancing in the light of the red candles, on the arm of some twenty-year-old mulatto. But whether love or sex, it's a definite reason if not a truly decisive one.

Take Kröger, a bigwig from Europe: he was supposed to have flown off to some conference in Brussels some time ago, but two weeks later, he's still here. In his mid-fifties, the father of a family, a distinguished-looking power broker—he no longer even opens his telegrams and orders his first rum punch at ten in the morning. Twice he got himself as far as the airport, but both times he had his bags sent back at the last minute. "I'll explain it to you later," he said, gracing the Hemingway types in the Oloffson bar with a wry smile.

And he did explain it to me later, in the buff next to the swimming pool, when there was really nothing left to explain. And Petit Pierre? It is he who now serves as Minister of Tourism, and one now finds him holding court in the bar at the Oloffson, filled with a happy fatalism that no longer has anything to do with alcohol.

Nothing could be more uncertain than the future of the tightrope walker Aubelin Jolicoeur, Minister of Tourism without a net—and without tourists. He bravely keeps playing backgammon with the boss-lady, bravely sips his drink, laced—as rum punch has always been—with a dash of fear for one's life, a splash of terror. Cheers, Petit Pierre!

P.S. Only a few weeks later, it happened that Aubelin Jolicoeur was relieved of his post as Minister of Tourism.

Citrus fruits come originally from East Asia. Lemons were first known in India, oranges in China, and grapefruit in Malaysia. They were carried to other tropical regions around the world over the centuries by Arab and European traders.

Lemons thrive in the subtropics, where they continually bear flowers, leaves, and fruit. They are harvested three times a year.

Oranges are second only to bananas in the international fruit trade. They come in countless different shapes and colors. Major varieties are the blood oranges, with either pinkish or deep red flesh, the blonde oranges, including the popular seedless variety known as navels, and green ones, which are found only in Sri Lanka. Oranges are grown not only in the tropics, but also in moderate climates like those of California, Florida, and the Mediterranean. Introduced to Europe by the Portuguese, orange trees became the rage during the Baroque era; every palace of any pretensions had to have its *orangerie*, where the ornamental plants were housed through the winter.

The first grapefruit to be harvested in the Caribbean were grown in Puerto Rico, in around 1750. It is thought that grapefruit are the result of crossing oranges with shaddock, a much larger citrus fruit with a very thick rind. Ninety percent of the world's grapefruit comes from the United States, where the fruit began to be cultivated only around the turn of the century.

Limes, a bitter fruit but the most important of the citrus family for the tropical bar, are much more popular in America than in Europe. Known as the lemon of the tropics, the lime is smaller than a lemon and usually absolutely round. When half ripe it is green, but when fully ripened it lightens to a yellow-green or yellow. It grows on small trees with prickly branches, and its pulp is more aromatic than that of the other citrus varieties.

Limes were first brought to Central America from East Asia by the Spanish in the sixteenth century. Today they are grown on all of the Caribbean islands, in Mexico, Brazil, Florida, and the tropical regions of Asia and Africa. The trees are often allowed to grow wild, competing for space with thickets of native shrubbery. Caribbean teenagers given to sneaking off to such thickets to flirt out of sight of their elders speak of such activity as "liming." For centuries, limes were of great importance to European seafarers: because they keep well and constitute a rich source of vitamin C, they were carried on long journeys to help prevent scurvy.

The pineapple, so named because of its resemblance to a large pinecone, is another staple in the tropical bar. This fruit was first discovered in the dry border region between Brazil, Argentina, and Paraguay. For export, the fruit is harvested green, because it continues to ripen during storage and transport. A new plant requires from two to three years to bear fruit—one of the reasons why pineapples tend to cost more than other exotic fruits.

The pineapple is actually a composite fruit. The stalk that bears it first produces over a hundred small purplish flowers. Each of these then matures into a small berry, and as these berries increase in size they fuse together, ultimately merging with the stalk itself. Pineapples are best grown on tropical bottomland, where they benefit from the constant warmth and humidity. Because they flourish so long as the temperature is steady, in Europe pineapples were cultivated in greenhouses as early as the eighteenth century. Even today, they are grown under glass commercially on the island of San Miguel in the Azores. More typically, one finds huge plantations of pineapples in all tropical regions of the globe. Hawaii proved to be an ideal environment for them and accounts for fully a third of the world's production.

Bananas are the great success story in the international fruit trade, but they are frequently a problem for the producing countries. Huge fruit cartels set prices and production quotas, and small Caribbean nations such as Grenada, Dominica, St. Vincent, and St. Lucia can barely afford to cultivate and harvest the fruit at current prices. Like many other tropical fruits, bananas were once confined to East Asia. The Portuguese introduced them to the Canary Islands in 1402, and soon took them to Central and South America as well. Bananas have been imported into Europe only since 1885.

Banana plants can grow to be over thirty feet tall, yet they are not actually trees but rather a relative of simple grasses. Their palmlike trunk is made up of leaf stalks, and is easily bent in a strong wind. A single plant can produce as many as 200 fruits in a mere fourteen weeks—a typical bunch weighing from 65 to 100 pounds. Moreover, it continues to produce year-round. All that it requires is a tropical climate with occasional heavy downpours.

Export bananas are picked while still green, each bunch being cut up into clusters, or "hands," of four to eight "fingers" of the fruit. These are then ripened in special warehouses in the importing country.

any tropical fruits are not suited for lengthy transport, and are known in the world's markets chiefly in the form of juice or syrup. Here, briefly, are some of the crops behind those exotic labels:

The papaya grows on a tree crowned by a palmlike roof of long-stemmed leaves. The fruits hang below this crown in a dense cluster around the trunk. Originally from southern Mexico, the papaya was introduced to Hawaii in the early nineteenth century. Today there are numerous varieties throughout the tropics and subtropics. The trees blossom and bear fruit all year long. In milder climates, these sweetish fruits with their gleaming yellow-pink flesh average about a pound in weight, whereas one can find them in the tropics growing to be five times as big. The unripe papaya is green; a fully ripened one is a golden yellow.

The guava is related to the evergreen myrtle—as are cloves, cinnamon, and nutmeg; even so, the guava is by no means spicy in taste. It is difficult to describe its flavor precisely. Experts call it "a harmonious blend of pear and fig, with a touch of strawberry." The most important guava-producing regions are in Mexico, Colombia, Brazil, India, South Africa, Australia, Hawaii, and the southernmost portions of the United States. In the orchard, the guava tree is rarely taller than a shrub. Its apple-size fruits have a light green or yellow rind. The flesh of the fruit is divided into four or five sections and contains many seeds, but these are perfectly edible. The guava of the Far East has white flesh and a milder flavor than the pink or reddish varieties grown in Australia or Hawaii. The Latin American guava has the most pungent aroma.

Almost totally unknown in northern climates is the prolific family of fruits called Annona. The largest of these can grow to be the size of a pumpkin and weigh up to fifteen pounds. It grows on an evergreen tree, is covered with spines, and is extremely perishable. This is the soursop, also known as *guanabana* in Spanish and *corossol épineux* in French. Despite its name, the fruit is not sour but quite mild in flavor. Pressed to form a thick, milky juice, it makes a refreshing and nourishing drink. Somewhat better known of late is the cherimoya, a type of Annona that grows in the Andes up to an altitude of five thousand feet and also in Israel and Spain. The cherimoya is normally about the size of a large grapefruit; its flesh is stringy,

whitish pink, and filled with black seeds. In the Caribbean it may weigh as much as eighteen pounds.

The most widespread member of the Annona family is the sugar apple or sweetsop. This fruit resembles an oversized pinecone, and when fully ripened it disintegrates. Somewhat sweeter than the cherimoya, it can be harvested green and stored until it ripens, by which time it has turned a brownish black. Because of its many seeds, the sweetsop is normally pressed into juice through a sieve.

The mango, according to the tireless reporter and frequent traveler to Mexico Egon Erwin Kisch, should not be attempted by finicky sorts. "Everything gets dirty: your nose, your cheeks, and your napkin, from which the spots will never come out." The reason? The huge pit of the mango is difficult to separate from the flesh, so that eating a fresh mango is indeed a messy business—hence its nickname "bathtub fruit." Nonetheless, the mango has long been a staple in the most discriminating tropical kitchens. Known in India over four thousand years ago, the mango was gradually introduced—primarily by the Portuguese—to every region of the tropics, from Africa to the Caribbean and from Brazil to Hawaii. The evergreen mango tree grows to a height of eighty feet. Its fruits are a longish oval in

shape, and vary in color from green to yellow to bright red. There are thousands of varieties, each with its own distinct flavor.

The maracuja —or granadilla— is becoming more familiar in northern climes as a direct result of the rage for tropical drinks. This yellow fruit, which is native to South America, the South Seas, and East Asia, is one of three varieties of passion fruit. In addition to the yellow maracuja there is the purple granadilla, which grows at higher altitudes, and the sweet granadilla. All are fruits of the well-known passion flower, so named because its cruciform pistil and its corona are suggestive of Christ's crown of thorns. The maracuja is round, weighs roughly a quarter of a pound, and has a peel as much as three-eighths of an inch thick. Its flavor is mildly sweet-sour, and the juice has such a high acid content and intense aroma that it is most often sweetened and diluted before being served. The juice bought in bottles is generally a blend of the three varieties.

Mrs. Copperfield went over to a bench in the corner and lay down. She shut her eyes and smiled.

"That's the best thing for her," said Mrs. Quill to Toby. "She's a nice woman, a dear sweet woman, and she's had a little too much to drink. Pacifica, she can really take care of herself like she says. I've seen her drink as much as a man, but with her it's different. As I said, she's had all the experience in the world. Now, Mrs. Copperfield and me, we have to watch ourselves more carefully or else have some nice man watching out for us."

"Yeah," said Toby, twisting around on his stool. "Bartender, another gin. You want one, don't you?" he asked Mrs. Quill.

"Yes, if you'll watch out for me."

"Sure I will. I'll even take you home in my arms if you fall down."

"Oh, no." Mrs. Quill giggled and flushed. "You wouldn't try that, young man. I'm heavy, you know."

"Yeah. . . . Say—"

"Yes?"

"Would you mind telling me something?"

"I'd be delighted to tell you anything you'd like to hear."

"How is it you ain't never bothered to fix this place up?"

"Oh, dear, isn't it awful? I've always promised myself I would and I never get around to it."

"No dough?" asked Toby. Mrs. Quill looked vague. "Haven't you got no money to fix it up with?" he repeated.

"Oh yes, certainly I have." Mrs. Quill looked around at the bar. "I even have some things upstairs that I always promised myself to hang up on the walls here. Everything is so dirty, isn't it? I feel ashamed."

"No, no," said Toby impatiently. He was now very animated. "That ain't what I mean at all."

Mrs. Quill smiled at him sweetly.

"Listen," said Toby, "I been handlin'

restaurants and bars and clubs all my life, and I can make them go."

"I'm certain that you can."

"I'm tellin' you that I can. Listen, let's get out of here; let's go some place else where we can really talk. Any place in town you name I'll take you to. It's worth it to me and it'll be worth it to you even more. You'll see. We can have more to drink or maybe a little bite to eat. Listen"—he grabbed hold of Mrs. Quill's upper arm—"would you like to go to the Hotel Washington?"

At first Mrs. Quill did not react, but when she realized what he had said, she answered that she would enjoy it very much, in a voice trembling with emotion. Toby jumped off the stool, pulled his hat down over his face, and started walking out of the bar, saying: "Come on, then," over his shoulder to Mrs. Quill. He looked annoyed but resolute. . . .

They got into a hack and started for the hotel. Toby was silent. He sprawled way back in his seat and lighted a cigar.

"I regret that automobiles were ever invented," said Mrs. Quill.

"You'd go crazy tryin' to get from one place to another if they wasn't."

"Oh, no. I always take my time. There isn't anything that can't wait."

"That's what you think," said Toby in a surly tone of voice, sensing that this was just the thing that he would have to combat in Mrs. Quill. "It's just that extra second that makes Man O'War or any other horse come in first," he said.

"Well, life isn't a horse race."

"Nowadays that's just what life is."

"Well, not for me," said Mrs. Quill.

Toby was disgusted.

The walk which led up to the veranda of the Hotel Washington was lined with African date-palms. The hotel itself was very impressive. They descended from the carriage. Toby stood in the middle of the walk between the scraping palms and looked towards the hotel. It was all lighted up. Mrs. Quill stood beside Toby.

"I'll bet they soak you for drinks in there," said Toby. "I'll bet they make two hundred per cent profit."

"Oh, please," said Mrs. Quill, "if you don't feel you can afford it let's take a carriage and go back. The ride is so pleasant anyway." Her heart was beating very quickly.

"Don't be a God-damn fool!" Toby said to her, and they headed for the hotel.

The floor in the lobby was of imitation yellow marble. There was a magazine stand in one corner where the guests were able to buy chewing gum and picture postcards, maps, and souvenirs. Mrs. Quill felt as though she had just come off a ship. She wandered about in circles, but Toby went straight up to the man behind the magazine stand and asked him where he could get a drink. He suggested to Toby that they go out on the terrace.

"It's generally where everyone goes," he said.

They were seated at a table on the edge of the terrace, and they had a very nice view of a stretch of beach and the sea.

Between them on the table there was a little lamp with a rose-colored shade. Toby began at once to twirl the lamp shade. His cigar by now was very short and very wet.

Here and there on the terrace small groups of people were talking together in low voices.

"Dead!" said Toby.

"Oh, I think it's lovely," said Mrs. Quill. She was shivering a little, as the wind kept blowing over her shoulder, and it was a good deal cooler than in Colon.

A waiter was standing beside them with his pencil poised in the air waiting for an order.

"What do you want?" asked Toby.

"What would you suggest, young man, that's really delicious?" said Mrs. Quill, turning to the waiter.

"Fruit punch à la Washington Hotel," said the waiter abruptly.

"That *does* sound good."

"O.K.," said Toby, "bring one of them and a straight rye for me."

When Mrs. Quill had sipped quite a bit of her drink Toby spoke to her. "So you got the dough, but you never bothered to fix it up."

"Mmmmmm!" said Mrs. Quill. "They've got every kind of fruit in the world in this drink. I'm afraid I'm behaving just like a baby, but there's no one who likes the good things in this world better than me. Of course, I've never had to do without them, you know."

"You don't call livin' the way you're livin' havin' the good things in life, do you?" said Toby.

"I live much better than you think. How do you know how I live?"

"Well, you could have more style," said Toby, "and you could have that easy. I mean the place could be better very easy."

"It probably would be easy, wouldn't it?"

"Yeah." Toby waited to see if she would say anything more by herself before he addressed her again.

"Take all these people here," said Mrs. Quill. "There aren't many of them, but you'd think they'd all get together instead of staying in twos and threes. As long as they're all living here in this gorgeous hotel, you'd think they'd have on their ball dresses and be having a wonderful time every minute, instead of looking out over the terrace or reading. You'd think they'd always be dressed up to the hilt and flirting together instead of wearing those plain clothes."

"They got on sport clothes," said Toby. "They don't want to be bothered dressin'. They probably come here for a rest. They're probably business people. Maybe some of them belong to society. They got to

82

rest too. They got so many places they got to show up at when they're home."

"Well, I wouldn't pay out all that money just to rest. I'd stay in my own house."

"It don't make no difference. They got plenty."

"That's true enough. Isn't it sad?"

"I don't see nothin' sad about it. What looks sad to me," said Toby, leaning way over and crushing his cigar out in the ashtray, "what looks sad to me is that you've got that bar and hotel set-up and you ain't makin' enough money on it."

"Yes, isn't it terrible?"

"I like you and I don't like to see you not gettin' what you could." He took hold of her hand with a certain amount of gentleness. "Now, I know what to do with your place. Like I told you before. Do you remember what I told you before?"

"Well, you've told me so many things."

"I'll tell you again. I've been working with restaurants and bars and hotels all my life and makin' them go. I said makin' them go. If I had the dough right now, if it wasn't that I'm short because I had to help my brother and his family out of a jam, I'd take my own dough before you could say Jack Robinson and sink it into your joint and fix it up. I know that I'd get it right back anyway, so it wouldn't be no act of charity."

"Certainly it wouldn't," said Mrs. Quill. Her head was swaying gently from side to side. She looked at Toby with luminous eyes.

"Well, I got to go easy now until next October, when I got a big contract comin'. A contract with a chain. I could use a little money now, but that ain't the point."

"Don't bother to explain, Toby," said Mrs. Quill.

"What do you mean, don't bother to explain? Ain't you interested in what I've got to tell you?"

"Toby, I'm interested in every word you have to say. But you must not worry about the drinks. Your friend Flora Quill tells you that you needn't worry. We're out to enjoy ourselves and Heaven knows we're going to, aren't we, Toby?"

"Yeah, but just let me explain this to you. I think the reason you ain't done nothin' about the place is because you didn't know where to begin, maybe. Understand? You don't know the ropes. Now, I know all about gettin' orchestras and carpenters and waiters, cheap. I know how to do all that. You got a name, and lots of people like to come there even now because they can go right from the bar upstairs. Pacifica is a big item because she knows every bloke in town and they like her and they trust her. The trouble is, you ain't got no atmosphere, no bright lights, no dancin'. It ain't pretty or big enough. People go to the other places and then they come to your place late. Just before they go to bed. If I was you, I'd turn over in my grave. It's the other guys that are gettin' the meat. You only get a little bit. What's left near the bone, see?"

"The meat nearest the bone is the sweetest," said Mrs. Quill.

"Hey, is there any use my talkin' to you or are you gonna be silly? I'm serious. Now, you got some money in the bank. You got money in the bank, ain't you?"

"Yes, I've got money in the bank," said Mrs. Quill.

"O.K. Well, you let me help you fix up the joint. I'll take everything off your hands. All you got to do is lie back and

enjoy the haul."

"Nonsense," said Mrs. Quill.

"Now come on," said Toby, beginning to get angry. "I'm not askin' you for nothin' except maybe a little percentage in the place and a little cash to pay expenses for a while. I can do it all for you cheap and quick and I can manage the joint for you so that it won't cost you much more than it's costin' you now."

"But I think that's wonderful, Toby. I think it's so wonderful."

"You don't have to tell me it's wonderful. I know it's wonderful. It ain't wonderful, it's swell. It's marvelous. We ain't got no time to lose. Have another drink."

"Yes, yes."

"I'm spendin' my last cent on you," he said recklessly.

Mrs. Quill was drunk by now and she just nodded her head.

"It's worth it." He sat back in his chair and studied the horizon. He was very busy calculating in his head. "What percentage in the place do you think I ought to get? Don't forget I'm gonna manage the whole thing for you for a year."

"Oh, dear," said Mrs. Quill, "I'm sure I haven't got any idea." She smiled at him blissfully.

"O.K. How much advance will you give me just so I can stay on here until I get the place goin'?"

"I don't know."

"Well, we'll figure it this way," said

Toby cautiously. He was not sure yet that he had taken the right move. "We'll figure it this way. I don't want you to do more than you can. I want to go in this deal with you. You tell me how much money you got in the bank. Then I'll figure out how much fixin' the place up will cost you and then how much I think is a minimum for me. If you ain't got much I'm not gonna let you go busted. You be honest with me and I'll be honest with you."

"Toby," said Mrs. Quill seriously, "don't you think I'm an honest woman?"

"What the hell," said Toby, "do you think I'd put a proposition like that to you if I didn't think you were?"

"No, I guess you wouldn't," said Mrs. Quill sadly.

"How much you got?" asked Toby, looking at her intently.

"What?" asked Mrs. Quill.

"How much money you got in the bank?"

"I'll show you, Toby. I'll show you right away." She started to fumble in her big black leather pocketbook.

Toby had his jaw locked and his eyes averted from the face of Mrs. Quill.

"Messy—messy—messy," Mrs. Quill was saying. "I have everything in this pocketbook but the kitchen stove."

There was a very still look in Toby's eyes as he stared first at the water and then at the palm trees. He considered that he had already won, and he was beginning to wonder whether or not it was really a good thing.

"Dear me," said Mrs. Quill, "I live just like a gypsy. Twenty-two fifty in the bank and I don't even care."

Toby snatched the book from her hands. When he saw that the balance was marked twenty-two dollars and fifty cents, he rose to his feet and, clutching his napkin in one hand and his hat in the other, he walked off the terrace.

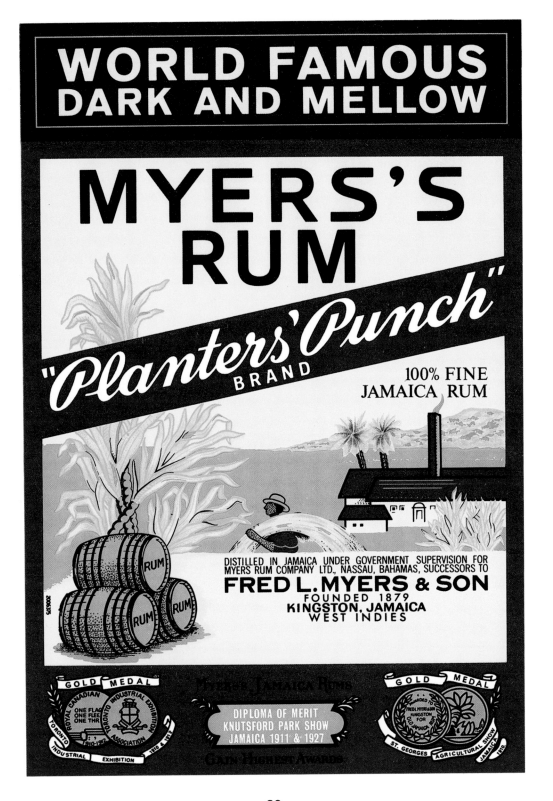

Planter's Punch, the most famous of all fruit punches, has been around since the seventeenth century. Some contend that it was the favorite drink of the colonial planters, while others insist that it was mixed, literally in buckets, and served as a refreshment to the slaves on the sugarcane plantations. Given what we know of slavery in the Caribbean, it would seem that the latter is highly unlikely; one cannot imagine that any of those plantation owners would have taken the trouble to mix punch for their cane-cutters.

Today there are countless variations on Planter's Punch, but it continues to be a combination of fruit juice and rum. In most of the Caribbean it is traditionally made with dark rum. On Martinique and Guadeloupe, however, in the French Antilles, they concoct their so-called *Planteur* out of white *rhum*—usually the brand known as La Mauny—and lime, orange, maracuja, or grapefruit juice. Another specialty of the French Antilles is *Petite Punch* or *Ponche Blanche*—equal parts of white rum and sugarcane syrup, a slice of lime, and ice. In the fishermen's bars on the coast of Martinique, the *Ponche Blanche* is actually slightly simpler and more effective. There it is simply a tumbler of white rum to which two spoonfuls of brown sugar and a wedge of lime have been added. A tried-and-true antidote to the hangover next morning is a plate of salted fish.

Other fruit punches may be contrived with the addition of whatever fruit juices are available, for example orange, pineapple, or maracuja. You can also combine several different juices in a single punch.

PLANTER'S PUNCH (1)

3 or 4 ice cubes

¾ oz. lemon juice

¼ to ½ oz. grenadine

2¾ oz. orange juice

2 oz. Jamaican brown rum

Mix in a shaker. Serve with ice in a highball glass. Garnish with an orange slice and a maraschino cherry.

PLANTER'S PUNCH (2)

3 or 4 ice cubes

¾ oz. lemon juice

¼ to ½ oz. grenadine

1½ oz. orange juice

1½ oz. pineapple juice

2 oz. Jamaican brown rum

Mix as Planter's Punch (1).

WEST INDIAN PUNCH

crushed ice

juice of ½ lime

1 oz. pineapple juice

1 oz. orange juice

¾ oz. banana liqueur

2 oz. brown rum

nutmeg

Mix in a shaker with 1 scoop crushed ice, and strain into a highball glass. Fill the glass with fresh crushed ice, and top with grated nutmeg.

RUM RUNNER   *1986

3 or 4 ice cubes

juice of ½ lime

a few splashes of Angostura

¼ oz. sugar syrup

2¾ oz. pineapple juice

1 oz. white rum

1 oz. brown rum

Mix as Planter's Punch (1).

YELLOW BIRD (1)

crushed ice

juice of ½ lime or lemon

1½ oz. orange juice

¼ oz. Tia Maria

1 oz. white rum

1 oz. Jamaican brown rum

Mix in a shaker with 1 scoop crushed ice. Strain into a highball glass half filled with crushed ice. Garnish with a mint sprig and maraschino cherry.

SCORPION

crushed ice

juice of ½ lime or lemon

1½ oz. orange juice

¼ oz. triple sec

¾ oz. brandy

¾ oz. white rum

1½ oz. brown rum

Mix in a shaker with 1 scoop crushed ice. Strain into a highball glass half filled with fresh crushed ice. Garnish with a maraschino cherry.

YELLOW BIRD (2)

Prepare as Yellow Bird (1), but substitute Galliano for Tia Maria.

COLIBRI

3 or 4 ice cubes

2¾ oz. orange juice

a few splashes of Angostura

1 oz. white rum

¾ oz. brown rum

Mix in a highball glass; stir well.

HURRICANE

1 scoop crushed ice

juice of ½ lime

¾ oz. Rose's Lime Juice

¼ oz. maracuja syrup

¾ oz. pineapple juice

¾ oz. orange juice

¾ oz. white rum

1½ oz. Jamaican brown rum

Prepare as for the Scorpion. Garnish with a pineapple slice and a maraschino cherry.

LIGHTWEIGHT SAILOR *1986

crushed ice

juice of ½ lime or lemon

¾ oz. Rose's Lime Juice

¼ oz. sugar syrup

¾ oz. white rum

1 oz. brown rum

Mix vigorously in a shaker with 1 scoop crushed ice. Strain into an old fashioned glass half filled with fresh crushed ice. Add the wedge of a lime.

HEAVYWEIGHT SAILOR *1983

crushed ice

juice of ½ lime or lemon

1½ oz. Rose's Lime Juice

¼ oz. Tia Maria

¾ oz. white rum

1½ oz. brown rum

1½ oz. high-proof brown rum

Mix as for the Lightweight Sailor. Serve in a highball glass.

DEEP SEA DIVER *1984

crushed ice

juice of 1 lime or lemon

¼ oz. lime syrup

1 to 2 teaspoons sugar

¾ oz. Cointreau

¾ oz. white rum

2 oz. brown rum

2 oz. high-proof brown rum

Mix as for the Lightweight Sailor. Serve in a tall drink glass.

MAI TAI

crushed ice

juice of 1 lime

1 splash orgeat

1½ oz. Rose's Lime Juice

¼ oz. apricot brandy

2 oz. brown rum

¾ oz. high-proof brown rum

Mix in a shaker with 1 scoop crushed ice. Strain into a highball glass filled with fresh crushed ice. Squeeze the juice of a lime wedge on top, and garnish with a mint sprig.

ZOMBIE

crushed ice

1½ oz. lemon juice

¾ oz. blood orange juice

¾ oz. grenadine

¾ oz. Cherry Heering

¾ oz. white rum

2 oz. brown rum

¾ oz. high-proof brown rum

Mix in a shaker with 1 scoop crushed ice. Strain into a highball glass filled with fresh crushed ice. Garnish with an orange slice, maraschino cherry, and mint sprig.

LOFTUS SPECIAL   *1986

crushed ice

juice of 1½ limes

¾ oz. grenadine

¾ oz. Cherry Heering

¾ oz. apricot brandy

¾ oz. white rum

1½ oz. brown rum

1½ oz. high-proof brown rum

Mix and serve as for the Zombie.

JAMAICA FEVER *1982

crushed ice

juice of ½ lime or lemon

¾ oz. mango syrup

1½ oz. pineapple juice

¾ oz. brandy

1½ oz. brown rum

Mix in a shaker with 1 scoop crushed ice. Strain into a highball glass half filled with fresh crushed ice. Garnish with a maraschino cherry.

CASTRO COOLER

crushed ice

juice of ½ lime or lemon

¾ oz. Rose's Lime Juice

1½ oz. orange juice

¾ oz. calvados

1½ oz. golden rum

Mix as for the Jamaica Fever.

HONOLULU JUICER

crushed ice

juice of ½ lime or lemon

¾ oz. Rose's Lime Juice

2 oz. pineapple juice

¾ oz. brown rum

1½ oz. Southern Comfort

Mix as for the Jamaica Fever, but garnish with a pineapple slice and a maraschino cherry.

PINERITO

crushed ice

juice of ½ lime

¼ oz. grenadine

2¾ oz. grapefruit juice

2 oz. white rum

Mix as for the Jamaica Fever.

FRIDAY   * 1986

crushed ice

juice of ¼ lime

fruit of 1 mango or 2¾ oz. mango juice

¾ oz. mango syrup

¾ oz. white rum

Mix in a blender with 1 scoop crushed ice. Pour into a highball glass; fill with fresh crushed ice. Serve with a wedge of lime.

ROBINSON   * 1986

crushed ice

juice of ¼ lime

fruit of 1 papaya or 2¾ oz. papaya juice

¾ oz. sugar syrup

1 oz. white rum

1 oz. brown rum

Prepare as for the Friday.

PUNCH À LA WASHINGTON HOTEL   * 1986

crushed ice

juice of ½ lime

fruit of 1 passion fruit or 2¾ oz. maracuja juice

¾ oz. maracuja syrup

1 oz. white rum

1 oz. brown rum

Prepare as for the Friday.

GAUGUIN   * 1986

crushed ice

juice of ½ lime

¾ oz. Rose's Lime Juice

fruit of 1 cherimoya

1½ oz. white rum

Prepare as for the Friday.

Sugarcane grows in all tropical countries and is cultivated solely for the production of either sugar or rum. It is one of the panicle grasses and grows to a height of twenty feet.

Like bamboo, sugarcane is divided into short segments, each set off by a raised ring. Each of these rings sprouts a pointed leaf over three feet long.

The original home of sugarcane was either India or East Asia. As early as the second century B.C., it was learned in Europe that the sap of the plant could be crystallized into sugar. Travelers brought back reports of "a new kind of honey that can be made, without the aid of bees, from a type of reed growing in the warmest regions of Asia."

Up until the Middle Ages, sugar was known as *Sal indicum*, or the salt of India. At that time it was a sticky, yellowish-brown substance, just like the sugar sold in plastic bags in every grocery store in the Caribbean. After Europeans discovered America and that sugarcane grew very well on the islands, the Caribbean region, and later South America, became the chief sugar producers for the whole world.

The cane is still cut with a machete, as it has been from the beginning. In 1860, the British writer Richard Hughes visited a typical sugar plantation and described the process of sugar-making as follows: "The sugar sap runs through a wedge-shaped hole into the boiling area, where a negro adds to it a light solution of lime to cause it to granulate. Then it is emptied into large copper vats and placed over fires that devour whole stacks of cord-wood, trash, and crushed cane. A pair of negroes skims the seething vats with long-handled copper ladles, while their comrades sit about in a cloud of hot steam, chewing on bits of waste cane and lapping up sugar."

All over Central America today you come across former sugarcane fields lying fallow. Less costly beet sugar and the amount of energy required in boiling down the sugarcane sap have made sugarcane production unprofitable. St. Vincent only recently closed the last of its sugar mills; it cost them roughly fifty-five cents to produce a pound of sugar, yet the price on the world market is only eight cents.

Other Caribbean nations, notably the Dominican Republic, are experimenting with sugar factories that produce their own electrical energy. Begasse, the stringy substance remaining after the cane has been processed, provides fuel for these "sugar generators."

The coconut palm is part and parcel of everyone's Caribbean fantasies, yet it is by no means native to the region. How it got here is quite remarkable, for though explorers and traders had a great deal to do with the spread of other plants, this one got around by itself. Presumably, the coconut palm was originally a native of the islands in the South Seas. They only spread to the Caribbean islands, South America, and Africa as coconuts fell into the sea, were carried vast distances along the ocean currents, then washed up on these distant shores and sprouted.

In many tropical regions the coconut palm is called "the tree of life," for nearly every part of it is somehow useful to man. Its leaves make excellent thatch, its trunk provides wood for framing houses, and the coconut shells may be made into bowls or burned to make superb charcoal. The central ribs of the leaves make good firewood, while the fronds can be bundled together to make brooms or can be woven into baskets and handbags. Finally, the fibrous covering around the nut itself,

which in the younger fruit is filled with refreshing liquid and in the mature one a tasty white flesh—the orange-colored King Coconut is purely a drinking fruit and does not develop any meat—is ideal for making mats and carpets.

Sap from the flower stem of the coconut is vaguely sweet, and can be fermented into palm wine, or toddy. This is then distilled to make arrack. The young coconut palm takes six years to bloom. The nuts clustered in bunches at the base of its leaves ripen in six to eight months.

Until quite recently the flesh of the coconut served as a prime source of vegetable oil. Some fifteen years ago it was supplanted by the soybean. Yet even today, coconut oil continues to be used in making soaps, margarine, candles, sun creams, and medicinal salves.

And finally, the colada, the tropical drink that has conquered the world, would be unthinkable without coconut milk.

She found herself in a bar, or what she had learned was called a rum shop in the island. Dimly visible in the sunlight that entered with her as she pushed open the door and stood hesitantly peering in were three or four roughhewn wooden tables and chairs set out on a dirt floor and the glint of a few bottles on a shelf halfway across the room. There appeared to be no one around.

One of the tables and its rickety chairs stood within just feet of the doorway, and with her legs about to give way under her, Avey Johnson stumbled over to it and sank down. Bringing her elbows to rest on the table, she buried her throbbing forehead in her hands and closed her eyes. . . . Finally, the dizziness subsided enough for her to raise up and look around her.

Aside from the few tables and chairs there was not much else to be seen in the place. Midway across the room stood a scarred, worm-eaten counter, a gas lamp on top of it at one end and at the other a small cluster of jiggers and water glasses turned down on a tray. Where was the person who ran the place so that she might ask for a glass of water? A number of shelves behind the counter were bare except for a half-dozen small bottles of white rum. Behind the shelves a partition of palm leaves leaning upright against some sort of a support blocked off the other half of the room. . . .

"Hello, is there anyone around . . . ?" Her parched throat could scarcely manage the words.

She was about to call out again when a voice, sharp, thin, hoarse with age, came from behind the partition. "The place is closed, oui."

Moments later a stoop-shouldered old man with one leg shorter than the other limped from behind the screen of leaves, advanced as far as the counter and stood there peering irritably across at her. He was dressed in a tieless long-sleeved white shirt frayed at the collar and cuffs and a pair of shapeless black pants without a belt that were more a rusty brown than black. He was holding the jacket to the pants in his hands along with a needle and thread. He had apparently been quietly mending behind the partition while she had been sitting there.

"Is closed!" he repeated, and made to shoo her away with the jacket. . . .

"Yes, but is it all right if I just sit here for a few minutes anyway?" Her voice was as testy as his. "I won't trouble you for anything . . ." . . . "It's just that I walked all the way from my hotel at the other end of the beach and need to rest out of the sun for a while before starting back. I won't be long."

There was no indication that the man had heard her or, for that matter, that he had even seen her—really seen her—as yet. Because although his dimmed gaze was bent on her face and he was looking at her, it clearly hadn't registered with him that she was a stranger.

"I'll just be a few minutes."

He said nothing, only stood there. He was close to ninety perhaps, his eyes as shadowed as the light in the rum shop and the lines etched over his face like the scarification marks of a thousand tribes. His slight, winnowed frame scarcely seemed able to support the clothes he had on. Yet he had crossed the room just now with a forced vigor that denied both his age and infirmity. And his hands, large, tough-skinned, sinewy, looked powerful enough to pick up Avey Johnson still clinging to the chair and deposit her outside. . . .

"Any other day you could sit as long as you wanted, oui," he said. His voice had softened, his look was less harsh, but his eyes still had not yet taken in who she was. "But everybody knows that come this time of the year the place is closed. The excursion, oui!" he cried at her vacant look. "I's closed for the excursion. . . . A man lives in this place all year he must go look for his family. His old father and mother if they's still in life, and the rest of his people. . . . Is the Old Parents, oui," he said solemnly. "The Long-time People. Each year this time they does look for us to come and give them their remembrance.

"I tell you, you best remember them!" he cried, fixing Avey Johnson with a gaze that was slowly turning inward. . . .

"That's why," he continued humbly, "the first thing I do the minute I reach home is to roast an ear of corn just pick out from the ground and put it on a plate for them. And next to the plate I puts a lighted candle. Everybody does the same. Next thing I sprinkles a little rum outside the house. They likes that. And every year God send I holds a Big Drum for them.

"And who's the first one down on their knees then singing the 'Beg Pardon'? Who?" he cried, and immediately answered himself by shifting his weight to his shorter leg so that he appeared to drop all of a sudden to his knees. And as suddenly he began singing in a quavering, high-pitched voice, his eyes transfixed, *" 'Pa'doné mwê/Si mwê merité/Pini mwê . . .' "* His arms opened wide in a gesture of supplication: *" 'Si mwê merité/Pa'doné mwê . . .' " . . .*

His abbreviated arms with the powerful hands at the ends fell slowly to his side. He shifted back to his good leg, appeared to rise. "Down on my knees, oui, at the Big Drum, begging their pardon for whatever wrongs I might have done them unbeknownst during the year," he said, his gaze slowly returning from wherever it had gone. "Humph, you best beg them, if not they'll get vex and spoil up your life in a minute. They's not so nice, you see them there. And when it comes time at the Big Drum to dance their nation for them, I tries my best, never mind I'm scarce able with these hill-and-ditchy legs I got. The Old Parents! The Long-time People!" There was both fondness and dread in his voice. . . .

Then with the pride again—and this time it almost brought his bent shoulders straight: "I's a Chamba! From my father's side of the family. They was all Chambas. My mother now was a Manding and when they dance her nation I does a turn or two out in the ring so she won't feel I'm slighting her. But I must salute the Chambas first."

Suddenly he was leaning across the table, his unsettling eyes just inches from Avey Johnson's. "And what you is?"

His face was a dizzying blur. His smell a mix of old flesh, seldom worn clothes and his yeasty breath. She pulled back sharply and for a moment, overwhelmed, had to close her eyes.

"What's your nation?" he asked her, his manner curious, interested, even friendly all of a sudden. "Arada . . . ? Is you an Arada?" He waited. "Cromanti maybe . . . ?" And he again waited. "Yarraba then . . . ? Moko . . . ?"

On and on he recited the list of names, pausing after each one to give her time to answer.

"Temne . . . ? Is you a Temne maybe? Banda . . . ?"

What was the man going on about? What were these names? Each one made her head ache all the more. She thought she heard in them the faint rattle of the necklace of cowrie shells and amber Marion always wore. Africa? Did they have something to do with Africa? Senile. The man was senile. The minds of the old . . .

She darted a frightened glance toward the door: she might be safer out in the sun.

"Manding . . . ? Is you a Manding like my mother, maybe? The Long-foot people we calls them . . .

"Wait!"—a smile began to work its way through the maze of lines around his mouth—"don' tell me you's a Chamba like myself . . . ?"

He waited, the smile slowly emerging, his arms in the frayed shirt poised to open in a fraternal embrace.

Avey Johnson was shaking her head back and forth as if trying to clear it of the sound of his voice. "I . . . I don't know what you're talking about . . . what you're asking me . . ."

"I's asking if you's a Temne, Moko, Arada or what!" He had lost patience with her again.

"I'm a visitor, a tourist, just someone here for the day," she said lamely. "I was on the cruise ship that came in yesterday. I . . . I left it intending to fly home right away, but I missed the plane yesterday and had to stay over . . . I'm leaving this afternoon."

Then, as the man maintained his irritated silence: "I'm afraid you've mistaken me for someone from around here, or from one of the other islands . . . who might know what you're talking about. I'm from the States. New York . . ." And she repeated it, "New York."

He gave a sharp, disparaging wave of the hand. Nevertheless, the magical name

had its effect: his eyes came into focus. For the first time since he had planted himself across the table from her, the man was actually looking at her, actually registering the fact that she was a stranger and not just one of the local folk who had wandered in on the wrong day.

Frowning, wary suddenly, he examined in quick succession her face, her chemically straightened hair, the expensive linen shirtdress, the cobalt brilliance of the rings on her left hand. His eyes lingered for a long time on the rings, becoming strangely fearful, and then they closed.

There was a chair next to him at the table, and blindly pulling it out, he sank down and lowered his head.

"I has grands and great-grands born in that place I has never seen!" It was a bitter outburst. "Josephs who has never gone on the excursion! Who has never been to a Big Drum! Who don' know nothing 'bout the nation dance!"

He fell silent, but the angry bereavement in his voice hung on in the room, troubling the air and darkening the almost sacred light that filled the place. . . .

"I don't remember the last time I walked so much," she began after a time in the dazed, uncertain voice, her eyes abstracted. "I just kept going and going. I wasn't even aware of the sun until I was almost down at this end of the beach. And by then it was unbearable. . . .

"You see I haven't been feeling myself the past few days. I don't know what it is. Everything was going along fine, I was enjoying the cruise as usual, and then for no reason, two, three days ago, I began feeling strange. Not sick or anything, just 'off,' not myself. And then all kinds of odd things started happening. It became so upsetting I finally decided there wasn't any point continuing the trip, that I might as well leave and go home. That's why when the ship came in yesterday I got off . . .

"It was this dream I had!" The small part that was still her old self heard her declare, and was astonished. . . . From the moment she started recounting the dream his head had come up, his eyes had opened and he had begun quietly studying her from beneath his lowered brow. . . . There was no thought or image, no hidden turn of her mind he did not have access to. Those events of the past three days which she withheld or overlooked, the feelings she sought to mask, the meanings that were beyond her—he saw and understood them all from the look he bent on her.

". . . So I simply got up in the middle of the night and started packing," she was saying. "Just threw things into the suitcases like a crazy woman. And in the morning told the two friends I was traveling with I was leaving. One of them was furious with me. But there was nothing I could do about it. I wanted to go home . . . I was sure I'd get a flight out yesterday, but—did I mention it before?—I missed it, I was too late . . ."

Slowly he rose to his feet, a diminutive figure in a worn shirt and faded black pants, with a look like a laser beam. He used it now to examine her again, this time seeing her half-combed hair, the damp wrinkled dress and the self crouched like a bewildered child behind the vacant, tear-filled eyes. He saw how far she had come since leaving the ship and the distance she had yet to go, and he said in a voice that was all understanding, all compassion, "Wait here for me, oui. I gon' bring you a little something. You's not to leave yet."

Moving with the briskness that again denied his age and lameness, the man quickly crossed the room and dropped out of sight behind the counter. The jacket he had been mending lay where he had tossed it, near the tray of glasses. For a time he could be heard rummaging around and dragging what sounded like heavy objects over the floor. When he raised up he was holding a machete, and with the long blade gleaming in the dimness, he began hacking away at something hidden from sight below.

The hacking was followed by the sound of liquid being poured, as well as other small mysterious noises, and then he was hurrying back to the table bearing what looked like a glass of cloudy water in his oversized hands.

Without a word, but with the knowing and compassion in his eyes, he held the glass out to Avey Johnson across the table.

"Coconut water?" she asked, pausing after the first swallow. Her eyes were dry now, the tears having receded, but she still felt the numbness inside.

He nodded. "Fresh out of the shell."

"And . . . ?" She was frowning slightly.

"And a drop of rum, oui," he said. "But not from those bottles you see there," he dismissed with a wave the half-dozen bottles of white rum on the shelves across the room. "I put a little Jack Iron from Carriacou in yours. Is the best. I don' give that to everybody."

Rum and coconut water, a standard in the islands. She had had much stronger versions of it in other places. Nevertheless she almost instantly felt that first swallow of the drink soothe her parched throat and begin to circle her stomach like a ring of cool wet fire. Eagerly she raised her glass to her lips again. . . .

She was blind to both the man's smile and her hands clutching the glass. She was aware only of the effect the drink, for all its mildness, was having on her. In no more than seconds it had spread from her stomach out into the rest of her body, moving through her like the stream of cool dark air that had greeted her when she first entered the rum shop. Spilling into the dry river bed of her veins. Before she had finished half the glass, it had reached out to her dulled nerves, rousing and at the same time soothing them; and it was even causing the pall over her mind to lift again.

In the last few years, at Schumann's as everywhere else, coladas have come to be among the most popular mixed drinks, the favorite, of course, being the Piña Colada. Accordingly, they are here given a chapter of their own—the first time they have been so treated in a bar book.

The basic ingredients in coladas are rum, pineapple juice, and coconut cream. But interesting variations may be created by the substitution of other juices and the addition of various syrups or liqueurs. Adding Galliano, for example, or Tia Maria, cognac, the Brazilian sugarcane brandy Pitú, or the Mexican coffee liqueur Kahlúa gives you a drink that is altogether delightful.

Genuine coconut cream is the result of the first pressing of the coconut meat, and has a fat content of roughly 35 percent. Coconut milk is a combination of this cream and the product of the second pressing, mixed with warm water. Coconut milk is from 10 to 20 percent fat. The product you are likely to find for sale as "coconut cream" is more like coconut milk.

PIÑA COLADA (ORIGINAL VERSION)

1 scoop crushed ice

¾ oz. sweet cream

¾ oz. coconut cream

2 oz. pineapple juice

2 oz. white rum

Mix in a shaker or blender. Serve in a highball glass. (I frequently substitute brown rum for the white or equal parts of brown and white rum plus an additional ¾ oz. sweet cream.)

FLYING KANGAROO   *1979

1 scoop crushed ice

¼ oz. sweet cream

¾ oz. coconut cream

1½ oz. pineapple juice

¾ oz. orange juice

¼ oz. Galliano

1 oz. vodka

1 oz. white rum

Prepare and serve as for the Piña Colada.

SWIMMING POOL   *1979

1 scoop crushed ice

¼ oz. sweet cream

¾ oz. coconut cream

2 oz. pineapple juice

¾ oz. vodka

1½ oz. white rum

¼ oz. blue curaçao

Mix first six ingredients in a shaker or blender. Serve in a highball glass. Float the blue curaçao on top.

CHOCO COLADA   *1982

1 scoop crushed ice

1½ to 2 oz. sweet cream or milk

¾ oz. coconut cream

¾ oz. chocolate syrup

¼ oz. Tia Maria or Kahlúa

1½ oz. white rum

¼ oz. brown rum

Prepare as for the Piña Colada; sprinkle with chocolate shavings.

COLADAS

GOLDEN COLADA   *1983

1 scoop crushed ice

¼ oz. sweet cream

¾ oz. coconut cream

¾ oz. pineapple juice

1½ oz. orange juice

¼ oz. Galliano

¾ oz. white rum

1½ oz. brown rum

Mix in a shaker or blender. Serve in a highball glass.

FRENCH COLADA   *1982

1 scoop crushed ice

¾ oz. sweet cream

¾ oz. coconut cream

1½ oz. pineapple juice

a splash of cassis

¾ oz. cognac

1½ oz. white rum

Prepare as for the Golden Colada.

ITALIAN COLADA   *1986

1 scoop crushed ice

¾ oz. sweet cream

¼ oz. coconut cream

2 oz. pineapple juice

¼ oz. amaretto

1½ oz. white rum

Prepare as for the Golden Colada.

COLADA BRAZIL   *1986

1 scoop crushed ice

¾ oz. sweet cream

¾ oz. coconut cream

2 oz. pineapple juice

¾ oz. white rum

1½ oz. cachaça

Prepare as for the Golden Colada.

MEXICAN COLADA   *1986

1 scoop crushed ice

¾ oz. sweet cream

¼ oz. coconut cream

2 oz. pineapple juice

¾ oz. Kahlúa

1½ oz. tequila or mescal

Prepare as for the Golden Colada.

PINKY COLADA

1 scoop crushed ice

1½ oz. sweet cream or milk

¾ oz. coconut cream

¾ oz. grenadine

¾ oz. pineapple juice

2 oz. white rum

Prepare as for the Golden Colada.

ZICO   *1986

1 scoop crushed ice

juice of ¼ lime

¾ oz. coconut cream

2 oz. papaya juice

1 oz. white rum

1 oz. cachaça

Prepare as for the Golden Colada.

BELLEVUE   *1986

1 scoop crushed ice

¾ oz. coconut cream

¼ oz. lime syrup

2 oz. pineapple juice

¾ oz. Cointreau

1½ oz. white rum

Prepare as for the Golden Colada.

The fisherman's knife flashed in the afternoon sun as he scaled and gutted two plump sea mullets. He worked quickly, whipping the entrails into the air where they were caught by circling seabirds.

"Ivan, come yeh," Maas' Burt said.

"Yes, sah?"

The man looked at him closely. "So . . . you a Miss 'Mando granpickney? What a way you favor her to death? Ah want you to tek these two mullet to you granny, tell her Maas' Burt sen' dem wid respeck."

"T'ank you, sah." Ivan picked up the fish.

"Dudus, tek the sprats to the café. Tell Miss Ida Ah wi' see her later."

The fisherman picked up the big basket for the market and with a grunt heaved it onto his head. The two boys watched him walk down the beach, the heavy basket steady and unwavering over his erect back and strong ebony shoulders that gleamed in the sun. As he went clouds of smoke from his pipe billowed out around his head, and above him a couple of sea-hawks squeaked and gibbered, circled and dipped, but never had the nerve to actually steal a fish.

"You wan' come with me, Ivan?" Dudus asked.

"Where you going?"

"The café. You no hear whe' Pa say?"

Ivan hesitated. He was reluctant to end the warm, magical glow of the afternoon, but he knew it would take some time to get back up the hill to his home, and he didn't want night to catch him.

"Bet you nevah go a café yet? Come on man, Miss Ida have a music box up deh."

Dudus's manner was mysterious and somewhat superior as they made their way down the beach, slowly at first while he explained how Miss Ida had come from town to establish the first café ever known in the district, a place where some people went at night to drink rum and beer and to dance to calypso and other music that came over the music box. Dudus's eyes sparkled in his freckled brown face. "Some a the Christian people in Blue Bay, the postmistress and teacher wife and so, them no like Miss Ida." Here his eyes grew big and his voice sank in volume but increased in intensity. "Dem say she a *sportin' lady*." He peered at Ivan, nodding his head for emphasis.

"Oh," said Ivan, then aware of the inadequacy of his response, "that awright."

"Yes," said Dudus, "dass jus' whe' me father say too.". . .

"An' you know what?" Dudus said. "I love Miss Ida. When Ah get big Ah going to beg her."

"Beg her what?" Ivan demanded.

"Beg her what? Beg her what?" With each repetition Dudus's tone was more scornful and incredulous. "You say beg her what? To married, a course."

Properly chastened, Ivan said nothing. Look 'pon Dudus though? Talking about married! Who woulda want 'im with 'im face round and speckle like booby egg? Always acting like 'im nice jus' because 'im live a Blue Bay. Talking 'bout him going married sporting lady? Spitefully Ivan timed his move and gently nudged his friend's foot, tripping him and causing the pail of fish to spill onto the sand.

As they gathered them up and washed the sand off, he asked, "What's a sporting lady?"

"Wait?" Dudus said, twisting his face into a mask of astonishment and contempt. "You is a *bungo*? You no know what sporting woman is?"

"You know?" Ivan challenged.

Dudus shook his head in disbelief and lofty contempt, as though in wonder that anyone could be so backward as not to know what a sporting woman was, and even more incredible, could accuse him, Dudus, of a similar ignorance. He stalked off as though he couldn't condescend to entertain such impertinence.

"Ah notice you don't say nutten," Ivan crowed.

"Me no have time fe play with pickney." He flung the response over his shoulder without breaking either stride or dignity. That was too much for Ivan. First by calling him a *bungo*—an ignorant and unsophisticated country bumpkin—and now a child, Dudus was attacking both his wit and his maturity.

"Who you a call pickney?"

Something in Ivan's voice told Dudus he had better steer the conversation into other, less hazardous directions.

"Is only pickney don't know what sporting woman is—the best woman in dis worl'. Every man love a sporting woman, but is not every man dem love." He started to add, for emphasis and to strengthen what he felt might be some weakness in his explanation: "Is only pickney don't know that." But, as the people said, "Coward man keep sound bones," so he did not. In any event Ivan appeared if not entirely satisfied with the explanation, at least willing to let it drop. So they proceeded. . . .

Miss Ida's Rough Rider Café was definitely not what he had expected, but then what had he expected? Dudus's explanation hadn't been too exact. The café stood on the beach in a grove of coconut trees, the trunks of which were whitewashed to a height of about eight feet. It seemed like a huge building to him, and was open to the air with low cement-block walls from which jutted the posts holding up the thatch roof. The walls appeared multicolored and as the boys drew nearer Ivan could see that there were people painted on them; women in long brightly colored dresses danced with men in shirts equally bright against the white background. They were people such as he had never seen before: they were black but the lips and cheeks of the women were blood red and their shoes were green or yellow or blue, as were the men's. When they got closer Ivan saw the figures were all grinning, though the various positions in which they were frozen seemed to him difficult and even painful if not outright impossible.

"*TChuh,*" he exclaimed with an air of dismissal, "dem favor duppi."

"You is a real hillside bungo. After is not so duppi look."

"How you know whe' duppi look like? You ever seen one yet?"

"See dem yes," Dudus muttered as positively as he could.

"See what? You too lie. Whe' you ever see duppi?"

Dudus lie,
mouth dry,
suck matter
outa donkey eye.

Ivan sang tauntingly, savoring his small victory as they approached the entrance. He resolved to act as though cafés were

entirely commonplace in his experience, and maintained his posture of exaggerated nonchalance when they entered the cool dim room with its smooth concrete floor covered liberally with red ochre. After the warmth of the sand the floor felt cool and smooth underfoot; he had to resist an urge to slide over the strange surface.

The café had electricity and a row of colored bulbs ran down the middle of the room. On both sides were tables with chairs made of wooden kegs cut to leave a back rest and a seat. There was the sweet wet smell that Ivan associated with rum shops. At a table at the far back a group of men were playing checkers and drinking white rum.

"What you bwais want? Oh, is you Dudus." The voice came from a figure moving out from behind the bar and wiping her hands on a towel. "What you bring fe me?"

"Some fish me faddah sen', Miss Ida."

Even before Dudus spoke Ivan knew that this could only be Miss Ida. She was a woman, as were his grandmother and her friends, but there the similarity ended. He couldn't take his eyes off her. Her lips were red, and when she smiled, as she seemed to do a lot, there was a flash of gold. A thick wave of black hair swung down to her shoulders, which were bare. And what shoulders they were—wide, smooth, black—and below them, outlined clearly under a tight red blouse, depended two round outthrust globes

duppi—spirits of the dead

fighting against the fabric and coming to perfect points some distance in advance of the rest of her. When she walked her hips, which flared dramatically from a tightly belted waist, rolled with a majestic rhythm as though to call attention to themselves. And indeed, the checker game was temporarily suspended when she emerged from behind the bar.

"Lawd," one of the men breathed reverentially, but loud enough for the tribute to carry, "what a woman walk nice, sah?" He shook his head slowly in rapt devotion.

"Then, why 'im sen' you?" she asked Dudus. "'Im couldn't bring it himself?" She accompanied the question with a toss of her head and a low musical laugh.

"Him say him wi' see you later, mam," Dudus explained.

"An who this?" She nodded in Ivan's direction. "I don't believe I know this little man?"

Ivan's eyes had not left her face. He didn't think he could speak.

"Is mi friend, mam—" Dudus began, but Ivan's voice cut him off.

"Mi name Ivan, mam. But dem call me Rhygin."

"Oh Gawd," Miss Ida bellowed. "If Ah laugh Ah dead." Her laughter came from deep in her throat, loud and easy, filling every corner of the big room.

"Bwai can't even piss straight," one of the men said. "Talk 'bout 'im *rhygin*."

"Lawd, don't mek Ah laugh," Miss Ida implored. "Ah can't stan' it. What dem call you, sah?"

"Dem call me Rhygin," he said firmly.

"So . . . you *rhygin*?" Her voice was low and thoughtful, teasing as though she were contemplating this information. "Hm, Ah believe you too. If, ha ha, if you was little bigger Ah woulda have to see how *rhygin* you is. He he heeh. But look what I live to see, though eh?" And she dissolved in laughter again. "Both a you come on." She walked her swaying, sinuous walk back to a glass case on the bar. "I don't know when las' I laugh so good. Come yah, Maas' Rhygin; you too, Dudus. Ah must give *unu* something, eh?"

"Well—speak up," she commanded. "What you want? Unu want fish? Jerk pork? *Bullah*, coconut drops, *toto*?" As she spoke she indicated the goodies stacked in the case; small crisply fried fish, peppery and hot with the heads still on; a lump of pork, equally spicy, smoked black for days over a green wood fire; the sweet cakes known as *bullah* and *toto* and candy made from coconut. "Talk up, what unu want, Rhygin?" She chuckled over the name again and rescued them from the necessity of choice by loading a tin plate with pieces of everything in the case.

They sat at a table eating, shrewdly measuring the diminishing pile of food. Ivan was trying to decide between a large tempting fishhead or an equally attractive lump of candy. If Dudus went for a bullah, then he could have the fish, yet how to get the candy . . .

rhygin—lively, passionate; also, sexually provocative and aggressive

"But wait? How Ah could evah forget?" Miss Ida's voice from behind the bar cut into his calculations. "Two sporting man like unu can't eat without music, eh? Lawd!" She continued doing something to a little box behind the bar as she fussed at herself with a pretended distress that thoroughly amused the checker players. "Lawd but how Ah could forget eh? Missa Rhygin, you mustn't mind, y' hear, sah. Old age is a bad thing, it worse dan obeah. Gentlemen, you music."

And the café filled with music. Or rather, to Ivan, the café filled with Miss Ida around whom throbbing, heady, erotically insistent rhythms swirled and played. The big lady was light on her feet; the carnal exuberance of her breasts and hips seemed to engulf him. She seemed transfigured, not unlike the ladies at Miss 'Mando's pocomania meetings, but the dreamy expression on her face, the smile on her painted lips were not very spiritual. Nor was her sweet, heavy perfume as she danced around them. Ivan's senses were assaulted in a new way. This was city music, café music, the music of pleasure and fleshly delight, and Miss Ida was its incarnation. She was a dancer moving effortlessly with the melody, anticipating the brassy variations of the trombone, but always coming back to the heavy rolling drumbeat that seemed to drive and control the bumping, grinding motions of those massive, insistent hips.

Oh Miss Ida

Don't you lift up any widah!
Seem to me that you set pon glidah!
Oh Miss Ida . . .
You a real rough ridah.

With a final challenging, shuddering roll of her middle, Miss Ida's dance came to an end with the music. The café became quiet, echoingly quiet, as though some dynamic and elemental force had swept through and then was suddenly and abruptly gone.

"Ah see say you like that, eh Missa Rhygin?"

Ivan nodded his head, speechless.

"Come back when you get little bigger, and we wi' see how you can dance. I believes you going be a dancing man, ha hah." . . .

It was an excitement that was hard to control. He kept speeding up dangerously. His impulse was to shout into the valley just to hear the echoes come back, "Rhygin a go home to raas. Raas claat to raas, de bwai a go hoooome." The sunlight on the lush leaves was almost too intense.

As if under ganja, he saw the foliage vibrating in sharp rich shades of greens, blues, and even purples. It made him drunk. Energy rose in him. He had money in his pocket and was riding a new bike. Behind him he had gifts, on his back fine clothes. He was a genuine recording artist even though he had forgotten the proof. He saw it clearly in his mind. Maas' Nattie's house, the café. Maybe Dudus would be working on his father's boat in the cove and they could go out to the reefs. *Aiie*, but the district would talk about the homecoming for a long time. Maybe he could spend a few days, come down the big river beneath the silent green mountains again. . . . After that he didn't know. . . .

"Hol' down! But . . . dat a Blue Bay town roun' de corner? Dat can' right. How me coulda miss de turnoff? Not possible, man. But it was the town. Den, right yah is where de fishin' beach is. Where dah wall deh come from, an' all dem big rooftop? No, dat suppose to be de fishing beach. Maybe is not Blue Bay. I doan reach yet, dis mus' another town? Bwai, is coulden laas' I laas? See a gate coming up. Whe' de sign say?

Private Property
SUNSET COVE CONDOMINIUMS
soliciting forbidden

The gate was closed but he could see a white gravel driveway, mowed lawns and whitewashed villas behind hedges of flowering shrubs. His disorientation was complete. Nothing fit into his memory. Dat a de fisherman dem beach. Wha' kin' a raas private? he thought. He was both angry and frightened, and still not really sure he was in the right town. He kept going slowly, looking around trying to recognize something and to collect his scattered thoughts. He was quite dazed. Alright, he'd go to the café. That was around the next corner. Already he could catch glimpses of the trunks of the coconut trees. Alright, he'd find people he knew there. They would explain what that wall meant. He speeded up and turned the corner.

The little café was still nestled in the grove of tall trees on the narrow headland. Raas. Wha' happen to de tree dem—an' de beach who pave it? *Bumbo!* It was as if a huge machete from the sky had taken the tops of the trees, leaving the slender trunks standing like futile, mocking sentinels. The café was unchanged except that where there had been sandy beach there was now a tiled floor enclosed by a low wall. In this area, a group of white people reclined in long chairs. They had tall glasses at their elbows, wore swimsuits, and were turning red in the sun. He sat staring slack-jawed and uncomprehending at the scene. The only black face he saw belonged to a white jacketed waiter who emerged from the café with a tray. Alright, he'd go ask for Miss Ida. But somehow he knew he wouldn't find her there.

One of the world's great bars recently celebrated its hundredth birthday. After my last visit, I wrote of it as follows: "The traveler who steps into the Writers Bar of the Raffles Hotel in Singapore on any given afternoon subjects himself to one of the erotic delights of high European decadence. Many of those titillating Far Eastern tales by Somerset Maugham and Rudyard Kipling that robbed a generation of pubescent, upper-class European girls of their sleep happened to be set in this most legendary of Far Eastern hotels. Now, far from young and in possession of their own (usually inherited) money, these ladies regularly appear, a great deal of rouge on their cheeks, on pilgrimage to the scene of their adolescent fantasies.

"One only has to look like a European writer to attract their undivided attention. The waiter who brings your Gin Sling, the famous creation of the house, will still pause beneath the slowly circling ceiling fan to say, just as in the old stories, 'For you, Boss.' At this the ladies feel themselves transported to the jungle, and cut off their cultured small talk in secret expectation of imminent rape. . . ." The ladies, after all, were responsible for the creation of the Singapore Gin Sling as it is known today.

The original Gin Sling came into being as the result of an attempt to create a tropical mixed drink based on something other than rum. On their voyages of discovery to the ends of the earth, British seafarers took with them the drink they were used to at home: gin. But once in the Caribbean, they discovered rum, the native alcohol made from sugarcane. Suddenly rum became the basic liquid nourishment of the British navy and British merchant sailors, and continued to be for over two hundred years. They relied on a daily ration of it whether in the tropics or crossing the frigid North Atlantic.

Only on the opposite side of the globe from the Caribbean, namely in the Indian Ocean, did gin continue to hold its own.

To make it more appealing to more people, someone in Singapore created the original Gin Sling.

In that original version, the drink was wholly a masculine business: two ounces of gin (86 proof), a teaspoon of grenadine, the juice of one lemon, and a splash of water—all well shaken with ice.

When the Gin Sling made its appearance, most of the world thought of Singapore as only a dump in some faraway equatorial swamp. But thanks to the drink, which gin-drinking sailors soon introduced wherever they landed, interest in the place of its origin suddenly increased.

The setting was ready-made for writers, beginning with the city's exotic name—a case of mistaken identity. A certain Prince Sang Nila Utama came to the island from Sumatra in the thirteenth century. On his arrival, the first thing he saw was an exotic wild animal that he took to be a lion. Accordingly, he named the island *Singa Pura*, or "Lion Town."

But the lion could only have been a tiger.

Only in 1819 did the dump in some faraway equatorial swamp begin to rise up in the world, for in that year it was annexed to the British Crown by Sir Thomas Stamford Raffles. His stay there lasted only nine months, but in that time he managed to lay the foundations of the Singapore one sees today: a gigantic free port, the central point of transfer for goods from all over Southeast Asia, and the only cosmopolitan city lying directly on the equator.

With Raffles, and over the years immediately following, a host of interesting characters began to arrive, providing the raw material for later writers. Since the Crown chose to place its elite in more important outposts of the Empire, the officers sent to Singapore tended to be the sort they wished to be rid of at home, restless and full of eccentricities. The town's solid core of wealthy traders acted like a magnet for shiploads of thieves, swindlers, forgers, and professional killers. Opium dealers consorted with pirates, and the well-bred daughters of the colonial rulers surrendered to the erotic pressures of slender, brown island boys during the sweltering nights, while their fathers dallied with the native maidservants.

Raffles Hotel opened its doors in 1886. Originally it was merely an overflow guest house for Captain Dare, a British colonial officer whose army of friends could no longer be accommodated in his private bungalow. Captain Dare later sold the Raffles to two Armenian hoteliers, who soon turned the elegant landmark into a favorite rendezvous. The bar in the hotel came to be known as the Writers Bar as it became clear that a number of England's most respected writers liked to conjure up their stories there, using their own experiences in the bar and doing their writing in the hotel itself—Conrad, Kipling, Maugham, and Coward, celebrated chroniclers of the Empire. The faces of the heroes in their books bore the features of the men sipping drinks in the Writers Bar, and the tales were the histories of those same men.

In 1915, the bartender in the Writers Bar, Ngiang Tong Boon, recognized what countless other bartenders would later discover for themselves: if you can induce women to come into a bar, more men are sure to follow. So a drink was required that was fruity enough to appeal to ladies, and at the same time potent enough to unleash a degree of frivolity. From then on, solitary male drinkers learned to take notice whenever the drink being served next to them happened to be a Singapore Gin Sling.

Tong Boon concocted a mixture that many men found revolting: equal parts of gin and cherry liqueur, a small amount of Benedictine and Cointreau, pineapple juice and lime juice, with a splash of Angostura to give it a little zing.

From then on, the men in the Writers Bar switched to what their compatriots on the other side of the globe had been drinking all along: Caribbean rum. Connoisseurs among them would religiously stick to the maxim "Never more than two kinds of alcohol in a single drink," mixing their rum with rum—half white, half dark.

Even today the Writers Bar of the Raffles Hotel serves many more rum drinks than Singapore Gin Slings, even though the management does all it can to capitalize on the legend of the bartender Tong Boon and his famous creation. Writers and journalists automatically receive a twenty-percent discount in the Raffles, for the management insists that "great bars survive only if they are in league with literature." And they're right.

Only the more serious writers tend to tell the truth, which is that while the Writers Bar may still be a Mecca for cultivated drinkers around the world, the Singapore Gin Sling is not one of the drinks they come here for.

The increasing variety of tropical juices and syrups available makes it possible to create more and more exotic nonalcoholic tropical drinks. The main juices under consideration are maracuja, mango, and papaya juice—along with the standards: orange, grapefruit, and pineapple juice. The various syrups include lime, mango, coconut, mint, pineapple, banana, and grenadine.

The recipes suggested here are naturally subject to variation. You should be aware, however, that tropical syrups are highly sweetened, and more than a few drops will affect the flavor of a drink too much. Maracuja juice has the strongest flavor and tends to dominate other juices. Mango and papaya juice, by contrast, are delicate and less aromatic. They blend nicely with other juices, and also with milk.

COCONUT LIPS   *1982

crushed ice

1½ oz. sweet cream or milk

¾ oz. coconut cream

¾ oz. raspberry syrup

2 oz. pineapple juice

Mix in a shaker with 1 scoop crushed ice. Strain into a highball glass and fill with fresh crushed ice. Garnish with a pineapple slice and a maraschino cherry.

COCONUT BANANA   *1982

crushed ice

¾ oz. sweet cream

2 oz. milk

¾ oz. coconut cream

¾ oz. banana syrup

Mix and serve as for the Coconut Lips.

COCO CHOCO   *1982

crushed ice

3 oz. milk

¾ oz. sweet cream

1 oz. coconut cream

¾ oz. chocolate syrup

Mix as for the Coconut Lips. Decorate the top with chocolate shavings.

MARADONA   *1986

crushed ice

1½ oz. milk

3 oz. maracuja juice

¾ oz. maracuja syrup

Mix as for the Coconut Lips.

COCONUT KISS   *II 1986

crushed ice

1 oz. sweet cream

1 oz. coconut cream

2 oz. pineapple juice

a splash of grenadine

Mix as for the Coconut Lips.

ARTHUR & MARVIN SPECIAL   *1985/1986

crushed ice

3 oz. milk

¼ oz. lime syrup

¾ oz. mango syrup

a splash of grenadine

Mix as for the Coconut Lips.

Baby Love *1986

crushed ice

2 oz. coconut milk

2 oz. pineapple juice

¼ oz. banana syrup

Mix in a shaker with 1 scoop crushed ice. Strain into a highball glass and fill with fresh crushed ice.

Long Distance Runner *1986

crushed ice

2 pineapple rings

juice of ½ lime

2 oz. pineapple juice

¾ oz. maracuja syrup

Mix in a blender with 1 scoop crushed ice. Strain into a highball glass and fill with fresh crushed ice.

Pelican *1986

crushed ice

3 oz. grapefruit juice

¾ oz. lime syrup

¼ oz. grenadine

Mix as for the Baby Love.

Boris Good Night Cup *1986

crushed ice

1 banana, puréed

¾ oz. cream

1½ oz. pineapple juice

1½ oz. papaya juice

Mix as for the Long Distance Runner.

Grenadine syrup is an additive that has come to be indispensable, not only for its sweetness and flavor, but particularly on account of its intense red color. It is simply pomegranate juice boiled with sugar. The pomegranate was a sacred fruit to the Egyptians, and is now grown in warm regions all over the world. The chief source of pomegranates in Europe is the Spanish province of Granada, which long ago took its name from the fruit (Fr. *pomme de Grenade*). The tree, with its bright red blossoms, is prized by gardeners as an ornamental.

Pomegranates have a tough, thick skin that is green at first, but changes as it ripens to yellow, brown, and finally deep red. On the blossom end, the fruit retains a crown of six stiff sepals. Inside the fruit are hundreds of seeds covered with a jellylike, juicy coating; they look like nothing so much as red caviar. To extract the juice, you first have to roll the fruit well to soften it, then puncture it and place it in a press of some kind.

Another staple of the tropical bar, though not very well known in Europe, is the tamarind. This is a legume, a pod roughly eight inches long and covered with a velvety, rust-brown fuzz. Inside are as many as ten seeds embedded in a piquant, bittersweet pulp. A sour-tasting syrup is derived from this pulp, and it is also commonly used in making marmalade, chutney, and Worcestershire sauce.

Tamarinds contain a higher percentage of sugar than any fruit except dates. The evergreen trees on which they grow thrive under semiarid conditions and may reach one hundred feet tall. Caribbean natives knead tamarind pulp together with shredded coconut to make delicious pralines.

No bar can do without Angostura. A dash of this bitter mixture is used to top off manhattans, old fashioneds, and gin and champagne cocktails. The world-famous bitters is blended from a number of tropical herbs and spices and has an alcohol content of 44 percent. It was first developed by a Silesian dropout in 1824. The surgeon Johan G. B. Siegert served in Venezuela with Simón Bolívar's army of liberation, but left the army to take over a clinic in the town of Angostura on the Orinoco River. It was there that he brewed his first *amaro aromático* as a medication against stomach cramps and digestive disorders. The firm Siegert established has had a stormy history. It has been confiscated and forced to move from country to country, but continues to be run by the doctor's descendants. Today, Angostura is made in Trinidad.

A final essential additive is Tabasco sauce, which is used to provide countless drinks with a welcome zing. Compounded of red peppers, salt, and wine vinegar, it is produced in England according to a century-old recipe. In Louisiana, Tabasco is made from peppers tended by the same family for over a hundred years, and packaged as the famous McIlhenny brand.

As for spices, one is most important: nutmeg. A number of tropical drinks, Planter's Punch for example, are served with a bit of it grated on top. The nutmeg is not a true nut, but rather the pit of a fruit something like an apricot. The pit is covered with a lacy red net called the aril, which is dried for its own sake and ground to produce the flavoring mace.

The tiny Caribbean nation of Grenada is the world's largest producer of nutmeg.

To really enjoy a drink made with genuine Caribbean rum you have to drink it under palm trees. Old acquaintances like Planter's Punch or the more trendy Piña Colada are just the beginning; to really get things going you need a Jump Up and Kiss Me, a Harvey Wallbanger, a Mustique Whammy, or—the absolute killer—a Hurricane David.

My list of the nicest bars in the Grenadines is short but select. At the top is Basil's Bar on Mustique, built out on piles above the surf on the beach of this small island opposite Bequia. The owner, whose name really is Basil, also runs a very good restaurant—The Raft—and a highly popular open-air disco beneath swaying palms. It is obvious that he knows what a good cocktail is all about.

Among his simpler concoctions are the Mustique Sputnik of vodka, ice, and lemon rind, a Caribbean relative of the Gimlet made famous by Hemingway, or the Jump Up and Kiss Me, also vodka, with soda, grenadine, and ice. The rum drinks are more elaborate, as for example the Mustique Grin containing equal parts of rum and green crème de menthe, coconut cream, a small banana, and ice, all puréed in a blender. The Ambassador, of equal parts apricot brandy and Galliano, rum, topped off with pineapple juice and sugar to taste, and puréed in a blender with a small banana, can be a bit on the sweet side.

Drinks that don't require a blender are the Mustique Sunset: equal parts of rum and Tia Maria, lemon juice, sugar syrup, and egg white shaken with crushed ice; and the refreshing Basil's Highball: equal parts rum, gin, and Cointreau, lemon juice, and sugar syrup, topped off with beer.

Equally enjoyable is the Mustique Whammy, a mixture of rum, champagne, orange and lemon juice, and a dash of grenadine. The Hurricane David is only for those who know what they're doing: equal parts of vodka, white, and brown rum, a splash of sugar syrup, and a splash of crème de cacao. According to Basil, this is "guaranteed to blow you down," and in this case you can take him literally. If you are short of cash in this bar, rest easy. Basil takes plastic.

The Frangipani on Admiralty Bay in Bequia is one of the choice watering holes for the yachting set and serves as the social center of the island. Again, the bar is located right on the beach, beneath huge old palms. The place is most famous for its Piña Coladas: white rum, coconut syrup—or better yet, Piña Colada mix—pineapple juice, ice, and a splash of lemon juice.

To whet your whistle before graduating to a Piña Colada, you might try the Coco Maria's blend of white rum, coconut syrup, coffee, and crushed ice, with a splash of Angostura. Also quite good, though less exotic, is the Banana Daiquiri, white rum, lemon juice, some banana liqueur, sugar to taste, all puréed in a blender with ice and banana. If you're feeling hungry at the Frangipani and it is Thursday, you're in luck; they put on one of the best barbecues in the islands.

A bit further north, on St. Lucia's Marigot Bay, head for Doolittle's. The food there isn't bad, but again the specialty is their cocktails. To get your feet wet, I recommend the Black Banana: rum, milk, Tia Maria, and a banana, puréed with ice in the blender. A more refined variant of the familiar Planter's Punch is the Marigot Delight, which adds Galliano and coconut milk to the rum, grenadine, and orange juice, with lots of ice. For an experience, try the Rusty Screw: rum, Grand Marnier, and milk.

Of course, if you have had enough rum, you can always switch to a Harvey Wallbanger (vodka, Galliano, and orange juice).

Back to the Grenadines. The massive wooden bar beneath a ceiling of palm fronds on the hotel island of Petit St. Vincent is one of the finest spots in this part of the Caribbean. Alton B. Collis serves as bartender, and he definitely knows his business. On hot afternoons, when the sun is beating down on your head without mercy, you need his delicious and refreshing—nonalcoholic—Fruit Punch: grenadine, pineapple juice, orange juice, a splash of Piña Colada mix, and a banana, all puréed in a blender with ice. Or if you're ready to get a glow on for the evening, you might try the Banana Cow, which combines mild brown rum, Piña Colada mix, and two small bananas puréed with lots of ice and topped with a splash of Angostura and freshly grated nutmeg. This is Collis's own refinement of the Black Banana.

The *pièce de résistance*, however, and the drink that Collis takes the greatest care with, even to decorate to perfection, is the Russian Satellite. This sledgehammer is Collis's secret weapon, and he was most reluctant to give me the recipe. Here it is: pour white rum, crème de cacao, white crème de menthe, and a little milk into a cocktail shaker. Shake thoroughly with lots of ice. Pour into a large brandy glass, then carefully float a hefty dose of 150-proof rum on the surface. Dust with grated nutmeg. Sip. In no time at all you'll see how it got its name, for you really will be able to see satellites—perhaps Russian ones—streaking across the sky.

Carlton and Princess had come down the hill by way of the path trodden through dry, brown grass, past a herd of a few dozen tethered goats, whose udders were now only furrowed flaps of dangling skin. There hadn't been even a cloudburst for weeks, and everyone was afraid that it could turn out like the year before, when not a drop fell from the sky for eight months, leaving almost all of the cisterns empty, and many of the goats simply dried up like the prickly shrubs and the grass.

Once at the bottom, taking the walkway of brushed concrete slabs through the sand, Carlton and Princess had passed the gray-walled power station that provides the village, but not the houses up on the hill, with electricity. Its diesel motors had managed to drown out the bleating of the goats for a few moments. Then they had come to the intersection where a small, whitewashed stone building stood—or rather shook, rattled, and roared. For on this particular evening the Park East was not so much an ordinary bar with a concrete floor, liquor shelves, a cooler, a counter, and a handful of stools as it was a kind of room-size, furnished, walled-in radio, with the speakers turned inward. Reggae bass notes bounced off the walls, soca and calypso rhythms rose and fell, back and forth, until they spilled out the doors and swept out over the east side of the island. This was the first of the nine

nights of Christmas, known as nine mornings here on this two-mile-long strip of land straddling the 12th parallel, this island in the Grenadines on the edge of the Caribbean Sea. Carlton, a fisherman, had come here in order to be able to greet the morning sun through a fog of rum, Princess beside him as always, not saying a word, her smiling face tilted upward toward the sky. She was wearing her flowered dress, the only dress she owned.

A lot of people had gotten here first. There was little Lennart, for example, with his mirrored glasses and his swinging, loping gait, his massive chest thrust out in front of him. He had acquired his huge lung capacity through years of diving for conchs, those large shells with the shiny, pinkish-red lip that are found only at depths of from fifty to sixty-five feet.

The towering Kenneth was here too, his head freshly shaved. As always, he moved as though in slow motion—even the reggae and rum only succeeded in eliciting a lazy swaying from side to side. Once I accompanied Kenneth from the Destination Grocery to the pier, where he was to deliver a sack of limes. It took him an hour to cover those few hundred yards. Kenneth was constantly amazed; if he caught sight of a white child off of one of the yachts dragging along a set of bright-colored plastic beach toys instead of the sand-filled sardine can a local child might use, or if he saw a white woman tottering through the potholes of the village street on her high heels, he would stop and stare forever.

In the light of the rising moon I had also seen my friend Mary slip by in her white dress. Clearly she had left Edwin in their bright blue wooden shack on Big Sand, on the other side of the island, where in the evening, after a day of catching morays, hunting opossum, or pulling weeds under the coconut palms, he liked to light up some "real good weed" and listen to the waves breaking across the reef. Edwin, the eternal outsider among outsiders, one of the few surviving Black-Carib Indians.

The scrawny woman who was always the one to start the dancing I knew only by the name Grandma. She lived with her many children off behind the hill in a hurricane ruin. Phineas, looking inexpressibly sad as always, had had to come even further—two miles on foot through the 90-degree dusk from the other village on the opposite end of the island. "Takin' a cool walk," he said. He had used the road that is here a literal highway, winding high above the sea and its bays. On one side are the jagged volcanic snags of The Pinnacle and Mount Olympus—better known as Mount Pussy—on the other, only blue-green water and the silhouettes of low islands built up as luxurious retreats for rich whites. Phineas had tried living in New York for a few years but had finally come back, discouraged and re-

jected by the monstrous city, to be with his blind mother, tend his garden full of peavines, his papaya trees, and his charcoal-burning fireplace. I could rest assured that before the night was over he would once again tell me: "We do need a new concept of life."

There were crippled old people and straight young ones, drunks and teetotaling Rastas, weathered, gray old fishermen and handsome young idlers, flashy whores and straitlaced teenagers in white blouses, their kinky hair forced into braids. The old muscleman was there, the one who had once come up to me with his green plastic glass full of "local stuff," to let me know that here you really were somebody if you had lopped off a white man's head with your machete. And there was the cool cat who had stopped me one night on the village street, taking a toke from his glowing ganja spliff, to ask, "Can you tell me where it is written that one man has to work for another one?" I couldn't.

And lastly there was Tis. At one time he had been the teacher in the village school, at a salary of eighty EC dollars a month. Unable to live on that, he switched to killing sharks. He would stand barefoot on the reef and lure them close with bait, then stab at them with his knife until he could wrap them in his net. For this he was paid one EC dollar a pound. With his booming bass, Tis was better than anyone at reciting the poem by Christine David from the neighboring island:

Who am I, I'm looking for me . . .
Am I African? European? West Indian?
I don't want to be brainfed
By Mr. Fred . . .
I don't want to listen and bow
And say "Yes, Sir"
And "So says thou."

"Mr. Fred" is the local name for an American, a Frenchman, an Englishman—any man who's white. The only thing Mr. Fred has to offer the natives in this corner of the world is a free look at his luxury yacht, his cruise ship, or his charter four-masted Sea Cloud. Or perhaps the chance to clean the bungalows he rents to other Freds for $200 to $400 a night, or to pass the drinks at his Planter's Punch parties. Tis puts it this way: "The only chance they give us is the chance to wait on them again."

Once the sugarcane planters had fled, after the slaves were set free, a century of black solitude and undisturbed calm settled over these volcanic islands with their white coral beaches. The isolation was so deep that many of these splintered volcanoes without a trace of fresh water were written off as forgotten islands by the authorities that once had governed them. In the last twenty years, however, a new white culture has taken over, sometimes snatching whole islands, sometimes only clutching to a point of land or a strip of beach like a tick holding tight to a spot of skin. This culture has brought its bun-

galow hotels with bars set up in front of potted palms, its own electric generators, and its private desalination plants. In bad times, such as droughts, it has also brought a supply of bullets with which to protect its enclaves of well-being against the rage of the unarmed populace, the black have-nots from next door. For the same purpose, it has erected fences everywhere you look.

One such fence runs across the sand only a few yards behind the doors of the Park East, behind it the landing strip for small planes and the yacht club. And all through this nine-morning night, while the soca "Feelin' Hot Hot Hot" boomed out from the Park East and while inside the bar its owner, Benjamin Adams—known as Buffalo, or Uncle Benji—poured nearly as much rum down his own ample throat as into the glasses of his patrons and while Carlton emptied his flask of Mount Gay, Princess spun slowly by herself with her eyes closed, and around them the knot of thrashing bodies grew tighter, sweatier, and wilder—all the while, Christmas dinner was being served to the white devotees of this exclusive tropical paradise on the palm-lined, ocean-view terrace of the yacht club across the way. Below the terrace sharks swam in their own lighted pool, and to the side a steel band played, having a hard enough time of it thanks to the competing soca volleys from the Park East.

Any white person who comes here has

to decide whether he is going to identify with the people inside the fence or outside. I had been living outside for months now, had gone looking for green *leguanas* among the tangled branches of the bushes with Edwin, had eaten Mary's *callaloo* soup with pigs' tails in it, and like everyone else had gotten by on nothing but dried peas and rice for two weeks when the

mail boat that supplies the island with fresh vegetables and chicken legs failed to show up. I had sawed up the melon-size fruits of the calabash tree to turn them into drinking goblets and bathed with the frothy leaves of the *ochro* bush in seawater. And at night, under the palm trees at Big Sand, when the quarter moon lay thin and horizontal on a fluffy strip of cloud and Orion sparkled at the zenith with the Pleiades gleaming off to the west, I had listened to the legends about the man who could understand mules, and the one who could see through the darkness, and the one about the obeah spirits that hover among the hibiscus blooms in the night—all the while drinking rum with brown sugar until it seemed my hands could touch the horizon, my feet brush the bottom of the sea, and my head strike the Pleiades. And I had begun to understand what they mean here when they maintain that a man can scream—either for joy or in pain—without a sound crossing his lips.

Another rhythm had taken hold of me, the rhythm of the burgeoning grass after a downpour, of the zigzag forward progress of the land crabs beneath the air-roots of the mangroves, of the blackbirds rocking on sea-grape branches in the breeze. Perhaps my experience was something like that of Camus's troublesome hero Meursault, who discovered that it was only in Africa that he learned again what it was to take a simple walk, then to venture a few essential gestures, "laying his hand on a tree trunk, running along the beach to keep himself whole and alert." André Breton speaks of his experience of the tropics in Martinique as "vegetation mania," recalling that he would cry out, "Flowers big enough to sit on!"

I had also begun to sense the world view of these people, living with them in their tempo of slow steps, long gazes, and easy conversation. I had begun to empathize with the ones who tried to recover a bit of their traditional African identity as a means of escaping from the crushing weight of the white invasion with its endless dollars. They had already revived the

Big Drum ritual; the Beg Pardon dances of their slave ancestors from among the Kromantin from the Sudan or the Ibo and Manding from Nigeria; and the *Bele Kawe* or Chicken Dance from old Dahomey. As they danced, they would sing: *"Anti koro you na yeri o, koro koro, anti koro"*—thunder roll, lightning flash, rain fall. Such was their life.

These people had no interest in the ones across the way and their Christmas dinner, passing around their rum punch and awkwardly jumping about to the music of their steel band. They regarded them with a mixture of quiet respect and disdain. And in fact one does see, from the clearer perspective of one who has lived long enough outside the fence, how tense the wealthy white men are despite their luxurious leisure. The people from the shacks put it this way: "Them do not know makin' a real good life."

Buffalo Adams—Uncle Benji—was already lying with his head on the counter in a state of blissful intoxication when Louisa made her appearance on this nine-morning night. Louisa, probably the happiest whore in the world, was a woman who lived on both sides of the fence and whose motto read, simply, "What they don't give me, I take."

Louisa revived the evening with a few claps of her hands and the command "Let's dance!" The speakers again began to blare out "Tango in de Disco" and "Rum and Coca-Cola." Louisa stood in the cen-

ter of the room, her bare feet slapping the floor as her fat buttocks swayed from side to side. Immediately she was joined by a tangle of sweaty, thrusting bodies. Kenneth leaped up to become a part of it, Carlton as well, and the girls with the braids rushed forward, waving their arms above their heads and leading with their hips. Lennart pushed his massive chest into the midst of the throng, jerking his head with its mirrored glasses to the staccato beat filling the room. Princess turned in circles off to the side with her eyes closed and her arms spread wide, and Louisa screamed, "Come on, gimme your hips!" The hips ground and thrust as the speakers thundered "Push it, push it, push it to me!" Then suddenly a hissing, swishing sound drowned out the music; a curtain of falling water became visible through the doorways and the sand outside disappeared beneath a lake that flung back in splashing fountains the torrents of the tropical downpour.

At that moment, a huge black man I had never seen before staggered in through the watery curtain, took a long drink from the half-empty bottle of rum he was carrying, and fell over backwards onto the concrete, where he lay with a bleeding head and glazed eyes.

It was no big deal. After a pitcher of Nescafé he was back on his feet. But that spelled the end of the nine-morning night. The power station failed, and there was no more music. So everyone ran or reeled back to his house or his shack, passing the bleating goats overjoyed with the sudden wetness. The only lights still burning were those of the yacht club, thanks to its private generators. And its steel band continued to pound out "Miami Blue"—the clear victor in this night of noisemaking.

The next morning I ran into the giant again. His name was Russel, and he had a rowboat that he had made himself drawn up on the beach. He invited me to come visit him. I asked him where he lived and immediately he pointed to the east, out at the sea, where a tiny green spot of land was visible at the end of the reef, an islet no more than thirty feet in diameter. We rowed out to it.

Russel had moved out here away from everybody. He slept in a tent, carved coral jewelry, and sold it to tourists from the cruise ships. He no longer fit in anywhere else. He had been to sea for years, knew Caracas, London, Africa, and Asia, and no longer felt any pull to the country of his ancestors. Russel had begun to think like a white man.

In front of us the yachts bobbed up and down; behind us lay the great reef that closes off the Caribbean Sea to the east: World's End reef. "Look at those yachts," he commanded. "You're looking at millions of dollars. I don't have any money, but you do. Why don't you buy us some wood, a gas cooler, a lot of rum and juice, a couple of stools, some petroleum lamps, and a record player. We'll build ourselves

a bar here on my island. It could become a 'big thing'; they'll all come rowing over here from their yachts."

"We can call it the World's End Bar," I responded. "It will be the smallest, most unusual bar in the world."

Then we tried to imagine what it would be like to plant a few palms here on this little circle of land at the end of the world in the middle of the turquoise-colored water, to build a simple shack, start mixing drinks with rum, and grow rich. Some day we would buy ourselves a generator too, and a device for removing the salt from the seawater. And then we would build a fence around our place, because the guests wouldn't like it if the black kids started swimming over in packs from the village . . .

Three years later I went there again. Carlton was dead—a heart attack after a cold shower at the end of a hard, hot day of fishing for snappers, barracuda, and dolphins. Princess was working as a chambermaid in a bungalow hotel on another island. Buffalo Adams had succumbed after circulation trouble, and Tis had left for Trinidad.

An American woman had installed a cooler in the Park East, stocking fresh fruit and vegetables for the yacht club on the other side of the fence.

Russel was still out on his island. I swam out to see him, and once again we fantasized about the bar at the end of the world. But that is as far as we got.

Hot punches suddenly became extremely popular in England at the end of the seventeenth century. People would throw enormous punch parties to sample the latest recipe brought back by sailors from India. The largest on record was given by Admiral Edward Russell in the year 1694: six thousand guests helped drain a huge basin containing a mixture of eight barrels of rum, an equal amount of hot water, eighty quarts of lemon juice, three hundred pounds of sugar, ten kegs of Malaga wine, and five pounds of cinnamon. The word "punch" comes from the Hindu *pantscha*, meaning "five." Five was the number of elements required for the original concoction: fire, water, earth (sugar), air (spices), and spirit (rum).

Grog had been invented over fifty years earlier by the British admiral Edward Vernon, commander of the fleet in the West Indies. He hoped that sugared "rum water" would keep his sailors from drinking excessive amounts of straight rum. Vernon is supposed to have worn at all times a sea coat made out of a coarse cloth known as grogram, and the English sailors shortened the word as the name for his drink.

The ingredients of all hot punches and grogs should be heated only to the boiling point. Hot drinks should always be served in heatproof glass.

FISH HOUSE PUNCH (1)

(Schumann's variation)

grated peel and juice of 10 lemons

grated peel and juice of 10 limes

5 liters water

3⅓ cups brown sugar

Preparation: Squeeze the juice of the lemons and limes into the water and add the grated peel. Bring the water to a boil, stir in the brown sugar, and continue to boil until the liquid forms a syrup.
Add:
3 liters Jamaican brown rum

1 liter brandy

¼ flask Southern Comfort

Stir well and bring again to a boil. Serve immediately, or store in sealed jars.
Sealed jars can be stored for several days.

FISH HOUSE PUNCH (2)

Instead of 5 liters water, substitute 2 liters water and 3 liters black tea.

(Fish House Punch can be served either hot or cold. Serve hot in a heatproof punch glass. Cold: serve in a highball glass filled with crushed ice. Float ¼ oz. high-proof rum on top.)

HOT BUTTERED RUM

½ oz. sugar syrup or 2 teaspoons sugar

2 oz. Jamaican brown rum

hot water

Warm the rum in a nonreactive saucepan; add the sugar and stir until it dissolves. Pour the mixture into a heatproof punch glass and fill the glass with very hot water. Garnish with a pat of butter.

MARTIN'S RUM ORANGE PUNCH   *1982

1½ oz. orange juice

¾ oz. Rose's Lime Juice

juice of ½ lime

2 teaspoons sugar

¼ oz. Southern Comfort

¾ oz. high-proof brown rum

1½ oz. brown rum

Warm all the ingredients in a nonreactive saucepan. Serve in a heatproof punch glass. Garnish with wedges of lime and orange.

HOT JAMAICAN

½ oz. sugar syrup

juice of ½ lime

2 oz. Jamaican brown rum

boiling water

½ cinnamon stick

2 cloves

1 wedge of lime

Warm the sugar, lime juice, and rum in a nonreactive saucepan. Pour the mixture into a heatproof punch glass, then fill with boiling water. Garnish with the cinnamon stick and lime wedge studded with cloves.

TOM & JERRY

1 egg

1 to 2 teaspoons sugar

1½ oz. white rum

hot milk

Separate the egg yolk and white. Beat the egg yolk in a heatproof punch glass; beat the egg white separately. Add the sugar to the egg yolk, and stir until sugar is dissolved. Add the egg white and rum. Top with the hot milk. Stir thoroughly; garnish with grated nutmeg.

131

JEAN GABIN   *1986

1½ oz. brown rum

¾ oz. calvados

sugar syrup or maple syrup, to taste

hot milk

Warm the alcohols in a nonreactive saucepan. Pour the mixture into a heatproof punch glass, stir in the syrup, and fill with hot milk. Decorate with grated nutmeg on top.

GOLDIE   *1984

1½ oz. brown rum

¼ oz. Galliano

¼ oz. cream

1½ oz. milk

¾ oz. orange juice

1 to 2 teaspoons sugar

Stir the ingredients and warm in a nonreactive saucepan. Serve in a heatproof punch glass.

SWEET & HOT   *1984

1½ oz. brown rum

¾ oz. Kahlúa

¾ oz. cream

2 oz. milk

clove

lemon zest

Stir the ingredients and warm in a nonreactive saucepan. Serve in a heatproof punch glass.

HOT MM   *1983

1½ oz. brown rum

¾ oz. Tia Maria

2¾ oz. cream

1 to 2 teaspoons sugar

Stir the ingredients and warm in a nonreactive saucepan. Serve in a heatproof punch glass.

MEXICAN COFFEE (HOT)   *1982

1½ oz. golden tequila

¾ oz. Kahlúa

1 teaspoon brown sugar

1 cup hot strong coffee or espresso

Warm the alcohols in a nonreactive saucepan—do not boil—and dissolve the brown sugar in the heated mixture. Pour the mixture into a heatproof punch glass and fill with the hot coffee or espresso. Stir well. Top with lightly whipped cream.

BLACK MARIE (COLD & HOT)

crushed ice

¾ oz. brown rum

¾ oz. brandy

¼ oz. Tia Maria

1 cup of cold strong coffee

1 to 2 teaspoons sugar

Cold: Mix in a shaker with 1 scoop crushed ice. Strain into a highball glass and fill with fresh crushed ice. Hot: Omit the ice and prepare as for the Cuban Hot Coffee.

CUBAN HOT COFFEE   *1986

1 oz. golden rum

¼ oz. brown crème de cacao

1 teaspoon sugar

1 cup hot strong coffee

Prepare as for the Mexican Coffee, but omit the whipped cream.

PEPINO'S COFFEE (HOT) *II 1986

1½ oz. tequila

½ oz. Tia Maria

1 cup hot strong coffee

2 teaspoons brown sugar

Prepare as for the Mexican Coffee, topping with lightly whipped cream.

CAFÉ SAN JUAN (COLD)

3 or 4 ice cubes

2 oz. golden rum

1 cup cold strong coffee

Pour rum over ice cubes in a highball glass. Fill with the coffee and stir. Add a lemon twist and sweeten to taste.

Mescal," said the Consul. The main barroom of the Farolito was deserted. From a mirror behind the bar, that also reflected the door open to the square, his face silently glared at him, with stern, familiar foreboding.

Yet the place was not silent. It was filled by that ticking: the ticking of his watch, his heart, his conscience, a clock somewhere. There was a remote sound too, from far below, of rushing water, of subterranean collapse; and moreover he could still hear them, the bitter wounding accusations he had flung at his own misery, the voices as in argument, his own louder than the rest, mingling now with those other voices that seemed to be wailing from a distance distressfully: "Borracho, Borrachón, Borraaaacho!"

But one of these voices was like Yvonne's, pleading. He still felt her look, their look in the Salón Ofelia, behind him. Deliberately he shut out all thought of Yvonne. He drank two swift mescals: the voices ceased.

Sucking a lemon he took stock of his surroundings. The mescal, while it assuaged, slowed his mind; each object demanded some moments to impinge upon him. In one corner of the room sat a white rabbit eating an ear of Indian corn. It nibbled at the purple and black stops with an air of detachment, as though playing a musical instrument. Behind the bar hung, by a clamped swivel, a beautiful Oaxaqueñan gourd of mescal de olla, from which his drink had been measured. Ranged on either side stood bottles of Tenampa, Berreteaga, Tequila Añejo, Anís doble de Mallorca, a violet decanter of Henry Mallet's "delicioso licor," a flask of peppermint cordial, a tall voluted bottle of Anís del Mono, on the label of which a devil brandished a pitchfork. On the wide counter before him were saucers of toothpicks, chiles, lemons, a tumblerful of straws, crossed long spoons in a glass tankard. At one end large bulbous jars of many-colored aguardiente were set, raw alcohol with different flavours, in which citrus fruit rinds floated. An advertisement tacked by the mirror for last night's ball in Quauhnahuac caught his eye: *Hotel Bella Vista Gran Baile a Beneficio de la Cruz Roja. Los Mejores Artistas del radio en acción. No falte Vd.* A scorpion clung to the advertisement. The Consul noted all these things carefully. Drawing long sighs of icy relief, he even counted the toothpicks. He was safe here; this was the place he loved—sanctuary, the paradise of his despair.

The "barman"—the son of the Elephant—known as A Few Fleas, a small dark sickly-looking child, was glancing nearsightedly through horn-rimmed spectacles at a cartoon serial El Hijo del Diablo in a boys' magazine, *Ti-to*. As he read, muttering to himself, he ate chocolates. Returning another replenished glass of mescal to the Consul he slopped some on the bar. He went on reading without wiping it up, however, muttering, cramming himself with chocolate skulls bought for the Day of the Dead, chocolate skeletons, chocolate, yes, funeral wagons. The Consul pointed out the scorpion on the wall and the boy brushed it off with a vexed gesture: it was dead. A Few Fleas turned back to his story, muttering aloud thickly, "De pronto, Dalia vuelve en Sigrita llamando la atención de un guardia que pasea. ¡Suélteme! ¡Suélteme!"

Save me, thought the Consul vaguely, as the boy suddenly went out for change, suélteme, help: but maybe the scorpion, not wanting to be saved, had stung itself to death. He strolled across the room. After fruitlessly trying to make friends with the white rabbit, he approached the open window on his right. It was almost a sheer drop to the bottom of the ravine. What a dark, melancholy place! In Parián did Kubla Khan . . . And the crag was still there too—just as in Shelley or Calderon or both—the crag that couldn't make up its mind to crumble absolutely, it clung so, cleft, to me. The sheer height was terrifying, he thought, leaning outwards, looking sideways at the split rock and attempting to recall the passage in *The Cenci* that described the huge stack clinging to the mass of earth, as if resting on life, not afraid to fall, but darkening, just the same, where it would go if it went. It was a tremendous, an awful way down to the bottom. But it struck him he was not afraid to fall either. He traced mentally the barranca's circuitous abysmal path back through the country, through shattered mines, to his own garden, then saw himself standing again this morning with Yvonne outside the printer's shop, gazing at the picture of that other rock, La Despedida, the glacial rock crumbling among the wedding invitations in the shop window, the spinning flywheel behind. How long ago, how strange, how sad, remote as the memory of first love, even of his mother's death, it seemed; like some poor sorrow, this time without effort, Yvonne left his mind again.

Popocatepetl towered through the window, its immense flanks partly hidden by rolling thunderheads; its peak blocking the sky, it appeared almost right overhead, the barranca, the Farolito, directly beneath it. Under the volcano! It was not for nothing the ancients had placed Tartarus under Mt. Aetna, nor within it, the monster Typhoeus, with his hundred heads and—relatively—fearful eyes and voices.

Turning, the Consul took his drink over to the open door. A mercurochrome agony down the west. He stared out at Parián. There, beyond a grass plot, was the inevitable square with its little public garden. To the left, at the edge of the barranca, a soldier slept under a tree. Half facing him, to the right, on an incline, stood what seemed at first sight a ruined monastery or waterworks. This was the grey turreted barracks of the Military Police he had mentioned to Hugh as the reputed Union Militar headquarters. The building, which also included the prison, glowered at him with one eye, over an archway set in the forehead of its low façade: a clock pointing to six. On either side of the archway the barred windows in the Comisario de Policía and the Policía de Seguridad looked down on a group of soldiers talking, their bugles slung over their shoulders with bright green lariats. Other soldiers, puttees flapping, stumbled at sentry duty. Under the archway, in the entrance to the courtyard, a corporal was working at a table, on which stood an unlighted oil lamp. He was inscribing something in copperplate handwriting, the Consul knew, for his rather unsteady course hither—not so unsteady however as in the square at Quauhnahuac earlier, but still disgraceful—had brought him almost on top of him. Through the archway, grouped round the courtyard beyond, the Consul could make out dungeons with wooden bars like pigpens. In one of them a man was gesticulating. Elsewhere, to the left, were scattered huts of dark thatch, merging into the jungle which on all sides surrounded the town, glowing now in the unnatural livid light of approaching storm.

A Few Fleas having returned, the Consul went to the bar for his change. The boy, not hearing apparently, slopped some mescal into his glass from the beautiful gourd. Handing it back he upset the toothpicks. The Consul said nothing further about the change for the moment. However he made a mental note to order for his next drink something costing more than the fifty centavos he had already laid down. In this way he saw himself gradually recovering his money. He argued absurdly with himself that it was necessary to remain for this alone. He knew there was another reason yet couldn't place his finger on it. Every time the thought of Yvonne recurred to him he was aware of this. It seemed indeed then as though he must stay here for her sake, not because she would *follow* him here—no, she had

gone, he'd let her go finally now, Hugh might come, though never she, not this time, obviously she would return home and his mind could not travel beyond that point—but for something else. He saw his change lying on the counter, the price of the mescal not deducted from it. He pocketed it all and came to the door again. Now the situation was reversed; the boy would have to keep an eye on *him*. It lugubriously diverted him to imagine, for A Few Fleas' benefit, though half aware the preoccupied boy was not watching him at all, he had assumed the blue expression peculiar to a certain type of drunkard, tepid with two drinks grudgingly on credit, gazing out of an empty saloon, an expression that pretends he hopes help, any kind of help, may be on its way, friends, any kind of friends coming to rescue him. For him life is always just around the corner, in the form of another drink at a new bar. Yet he really wants none of these things. Abandoned by his friends, as they by him, he knows that nothing but the crushing look of a creditor lives round that corner. Neither has he fortified himself sufficiently to borrow more money, nor obtain more credit; nor does he like the liquor next door anyway. Why am I here, says the silence, what have I done, echoes the emptiness, why have I ruined myself in this wilful manner, chuckles the money in the till, why have I been so low, wheedles the thoroughfare, to which the only answer

was— The square gave him no answer. The little town, that had seemed empty, was filling up as evening wore on. Occasionally a moustachioed officer swaggered past, with a heavy gait, slapping his swagger stick on his leggings. People were returning from the cemeteries, though perhaps the procession would not pass for some time. A ragged platoon of soldiers were marching across the square. Bugles blared. The police too—those who were not on strike, or had been pretending to be on duty at the graves, or the deputies, it was not easy to get the distinction between the police and the military clear in one's mind either—had arrived in force. Con German friends, doubtless. The corporal was still writing at his table; it oddly reassured him. Two or three drinkers pushed their way past him into the Farolito, tasselled sombreros on the backs of their heads, holsters slapping their thighs. Two beggars had arrived and were taking up their posts outside the bar, under the tempestuous sky. One, legless, was dragging himself through the dust like a poor seal. But the other beggar, who boasted one leg, stood up stiffly, proudly, against the cantina wall as if waiting to be shot. Then this beggar with one leg leaned forward: he dropped a coin into the legless man's outstretched hand. There were tears in the first beggar's eyes. The Consul now observed that on his extreme right some unusual animals resembling geese, but large as camels, and skinless men, without heads, upon stilts, whose animated entrails jerked along the ground, were issuing out of the forest path the way he had come. He shut his eyes from this and when he opened them someone who looked like a policeman was leading a horse up the path, that was all. He laughed, despite the policeman, then stopped. For he saw that the face of the reclining beggar was slowly changing to Señora Gregorio's, and now in turn to his mother's face, upon which appeared an expression of infinite pity and supplication.

Closing his eyes again, standing there, glass in hand, he thought for a minute with a freezing detached almost amused calm of the dreadful night inevitably awaiting him whether he drank much more or not, his room shaking with daemonic orchestras, the snatches of fearful tumultuous sleep, interrupted by voices which were really dogs barking, or by his own name being continually repeated by imaginary parties arriving, the vicious shouting, the strumming, the slamming, the pounding, the battling with insolent archfiends, the avalanche breaking down the door, the proddings from under the bed, and always, outside, the cries, the wailing, the terrible music, the dark's spinets: he returned to the bar.

It was from the Francia, a nightmarish hotel with rooms like jail cells, a snot-colored Victorian glass roof, and a plastic skeleton floating in a slimy fishtank—a refuge for ghosts—that Malcolm Lowry used to stagger to the market three streets away, to Farolito's. Farolito's is long gone. Indeed, it was already padlocked and condemned in the 1940s when Lowry returned with his second wife, Marjorie. Today, there's still a gloomy bar by that name in Calle Murguia, as well as a cheap flea-bag hotel in Las Casas—which may explain the presence of so many blonde Viking types and so many Dutch tourists who seem to hang out next door at the awful cantina named Lupita.

The hotel Farolito and its many neighbors, which bear the names of saints, boast the same clientele as the myriad local mescal bars. These bars can be recognized by their swinging doors and also by a combination of instinct, smell, and noise. They all keep different hours, as irregular and complex as the neighborhood itself. The Dos Equis bar, for example, doesn't open until late in the evening, but it stays open until 8:00 A.M. when the crowd moves to the Superior bar, famous for its riotous clientele and its incredible collection of naked women. The most psychedelic by far is the Cartagena, which is best at twilight when the rays of the setting sun hit its sky blue façade, its dark blue window frames, and electric yellow doorway—colors that, combined with its intense fuchsia interior, are like a foretaste of what one is likely to drink, or experience, inside.

Further west there are bars that cater to hookers, and honky-tonk bars like Los Juncos or El Flor del Jazmin. This whole area is located smack in the center of a busy and heavily populated downtown, where long straight streets lined with iron shutters (they look like rows of garages) are filled with pharmacies, hair-dressing salons, the offices of seedy practitioners and chiropractors, hardware stores, motorcycle repair shops, and the storefronts of doctors advertising magical cures. And, of course, the mescal bars.

The mescal itself is often made elsewhere, out near Matatlàn for instance, a town twenty-five miles or so down the road. But each bar sells only one—its own—brand of mescal, which comes in three flavors: *pechuga* (yellow), *gusitano* (with a worm in it), and *minero* (colorless). Contrary to the amusing but slightly tedious cult that has grown up around the dubious *gusitano*, mescal-with-worm is by far the least popular flavor, for the good and simple reason that it is rarely bottled. Yes, at the Maguey Azul or Nectar de Macateca bars you will find rows of bottles with labels reading "Souvenir of Oaxaca," but in the real Oaxaca, mescal is usually purchased in cans, sometimes even in jerry cans. Most of these are plastic, and you bring yours in to be filled up through a funnel in the back room. The bums sprawled on the steps of San Juan de Dios sip their mescal out of used soft drink bottles. Trucks pull up outside El Famoso Mescal de Matatlàn and unload it in bulk, in vast and vaguely unsettling sky blue plastic containers.

But let's be frank: mescal is not the kind of beverage that has anything to do with age—unless we're talking about what it does to the drinker. A fairly impressive number of dwarfs, idiots, and goitrous human discards seem to hang around the Mina Hotel, sometimes literally "laid out" on the sidewalk. For informational purposes it should be noted that the most sought after mescal comes from Matatlàn and that *minero* is the type with the highest alcohol content. Each mescal outlet differs slightly from the other in the proof of the product it sells and in the addition of such subtle flavorings as apple, quince, or sugarcane to mescal's maguey base. We remain faithful to the bar called Las Lagrimas de Maguey, both for its vaguely Christian connotations and for its yellow-striped façade.

Oaxaca should be seen both from above and from within. From the roof of the Francia, Lowry used to ruminate on the Zapotecs of Monte Alban. After climbing back down to his room, he found (or imagined he found) a vulture perched on the edge of his sink. Today, if we visit the

Marques del Valle, the hotel on the Zocalo beside the Cathedral, the birds we will be far more likely to see are sparrows as they take off in unison at 5:30 in the evening, when the bugle sounds and the flags are lowered in the neighboring barracks. Oaxaca is a secretive town. Its façades and mean, narrow windows conceal pleasant and often rather magnificent patios, drenched in sunlight. The roofs are like elevated junkyards, covered with surrealistic stacks of discarded bathtubs, sinks, mattresses and springs, the skeletons of motorbikes, and other rubbish.

The day may begin at the Comparia. While waiting for the newsstand owners to open the bundles of papers and lay out their stock, we can stroll into the unpretentious church to see those who come to refresh themselves with St. Ignatius's water. "The water of St. Ignatius heals both the soul and the body." You are advised to drink it carefully, and not, please, to use your hand. Two cups and a banged-up plastic dipper hang from a chain. The clientele varies with the time of day and the service being held. A ragged peasant advances on his knees and, crossing himself, drinks a cupful. An elderly Indian woman arrives with a child in tow; together, they fill three Fanta bottles and leave. Their place is taken by the attractive and well-dressed cashier from the corner bank. All of them deposit money in St. Ignatius's box.

Outside, the members of the shoe-shine brigade have taken up their positions. Everybody, no matter how bedraggled, gets their shoes shined. It's like the ritual of the café and the cigarette. However, at this early hour the shoe shiners mostly hang around the newsstands. Not to read the headlines, but to devour the *policiacas*, the police sheets that are hung up with clothespins. Each newspaper—and their number approaches the farcical—has its court calendar section, which serves as a kind of police gazette or blotter. The *policiaca* put out by *El Nuevo Informador* has even gone so far as to feature drawings of cop and thief at the top of the page, two cartoon heads that are like reflections of Donald's nephews Huey and Louie, on the cover of the issue of *Disneylandia* hanging next to it. By checking out the daily police blotters you can keep track of the feats of the local Robin Hoods and know which drug dealer is still managing to evade the authorities. These inky sheets have such titles as *Carteles del Sur, El Sol de Oaxaca,* and *El Rotativo,* and the newsboys can't hand them out fast enough. Then it's time to move on to the market, if only to down a ritual glass of orange juice at Lupita's stand. Would you like that with one raw egg, or two?

On the terrace of Del Jardin, they're arguing about soccer, as usual, but you get the feeling that it's only a variation on a familiar and necessary exercise: here, people argue for the fun of it. Bearded students gesticulate excitedly through clouds of tobacco smoke, rubicund public officials discuss their latest deals. Young Indian girls move among the tables offering bouquets of gardenias to the tourists and to the almost totally male clientele. One of them carries her basket on her head with ancestral panache, but not without a touch of irony as well. She is wearing a denim jacket and chewing gum, which she pops in the face of a client who refuses to buy her flowers. Tired-looking ten-year-old kids offer boxes filled with hideous "native" wares. My next door neighbor at the Marques del Valle is their supplier—his room is piled high with the goods.

There is always something to look at in Oaxaca. Here, everyday life is just as much a source of pleasure as are the local monuments: that coil of garden hose in vivid green, white, and yellow gives as much pleasure as the gold leaf in San Domingo, the posters announcing the wrestling matches are as dramatic as the ones advertising the production of a play by Juan Rulfo at the Teatro Alcadia. I'll never see Supermouse or the Conde Brothers in a match at the 3 Missionaros, nor will I see Sputnik mix it up with Tatum or Gulliver. However, I'll always remember those names plastered on the walls in Oaxaca, like mysterious code words, feasts for the eye.

I met Hippolito at Bum Bum, a fast food joint. A soccer fan, he was on his way across the square to watch the game between Denmark and Germany on the television set at Del Jardin. Hippolito is an electrician by trade, a café waiter by necessity. He told me that the life of a soccer fan in Oaxaca is a hard one. Although the sport is very popular, and although Hippolito himself plays on one of the local teams, Oaxaca is only a second-division town and may even fall to third next year. The World Cup is an event for him, and he never misses one.

Like many here, Hippolito is unsatisfied but uncomplaining. According to him, the governor doesn't know how to do his job—a while ago he let the town of Puebla cut Oaxaca out of an opportunity, "a chance of a lifetime," to get a Volkswagen factory built here. In Oaxaca everything is small scale, from the modest furniture makers' shops to the plastics factory. And Hippolito has obviously fallen prey to the common Mexican cast of thought, one that the right wing parties exploit to the full: ambition is regarded as a character flaw, at the very least as a serious weakness. Nobody ever says, "That man will go far." They say, "He's just a dreamer." Will this ever change?

Every tequila is a mescal, but not every mescal is tequila. This is the simplest way to define the relationship between these two favorite Mexican spirits. Both are distilled from the sap obtained by grinding and heating the stalk of the maguey agave. This stalk, or heart, has the look of a pineapple once the agave leaves are cut off, and weighs between forty-five and two hundred and fifty pounds.

Tequila is only that agave distillate produced in the provinces of Nayarit, Colima, Guanajuato, Michoacan, and Jalisco, the last containing the city of Tequila. Most of the tequila comes from industrialized distilleries. Mescal, on the other hand, *mezcal* to the Mexicans, is frequently distilled even today in the traditional peasant manner over charcoal fires. The word *mezcal* derives from *metl*, the Indian word for agave. The most famous mescal comes from the province of Oaxaca.

The first Spanish conquerors in Mexico were quick to learn that the heart of the agave contained a sap that could be distilled. During the nineteenth century the spirits produced in Tequila gained a considerable reputation, and in 1873 there were already sixteen distilleries in the little town in the province of Jalisco. Today some 435 million agave plants are to be found in the landscape surrounding Tequila, all of them of the variety *maguey tequilana*, a type grown exclusively for the production of tequila. It requires from eight to ten years to mature. Fifteen pounds of stalk produce roughly a liter of tequila; the finished product has been distilled twice.

Fresh tequila, usually colorless, is sold as *tequila fino*. When aged in oak barrels for several years it takes on a yellow-gold color, at which point it becomes *finissimo tequila espuela*.

Mexico's true national drink, however, is pulque—made from the juice that pours out of the agave *maguey atrovirens* once you cut off the heart leaf. A plant can produce as much as eight liters of this *aguamiel* or "honey water" a day. The slightly alcoholic pulque is simply this sap once it has been fermented; it is not distilled like tequila and mescal. Pulque is not an invention of the colonial conquerors, but was drunk hundreds of years ago by the native Indians.

Tequila became popular outside Mexico only in the early fifties, at first in the United States and eventually in Europe as well. In no time, customers were won over by the best-known of the tequila drinks, the Margarita and the Tequila Sunrise.

MARGARITA

3 or 4 ice cubes, or 1 scoop crushed ice

¾ oz. lemon or lime juice

¾ oz. Cointreau

1½ oz. tequila

Mix in a shaker. Strain into an iced cocktail glass with a salted rim.

FROZEN MARGARITA

Mix the Margarita in a blender and serve in an iced cocktail glass with a salted rim.

FROZEN MATADOR   *1986

1 scoop crushed ice

juice of ½ lime

2 pineapple rings

1 teaspoon sugar

¼ oz. Cointreau

1¾ oz. tequila

Mix in a blender with the crushed ice. Pour into a highball glass filled with crushed ice.

STRAWBERRY MARGARITA

1 scoop crushed ice

¾ oz. lemon or lime juice

¼ oz. strawberry syrup or several fresh strawberries

¼ oz. Cointreau

1½ oz. tequila

Mix in a blender. Serve in an iced cocktail glass.

EL DIABOLO

crushed ice

½ lime

¾ oz. crème de cassis

1¾ oz. tequila

ginger ale

Fill a highball glass half full with crushed ice. Squeeze the lime juice over the ice, and add the lime half. Pour in the tequila and crème de cassis, and fill with ginger ale. Stir.

TEQUILA SUNRISE

crushed ice

2 oz. tequila

¼ oz. grenadine

3 oz. orange juice

Fill a tall drink glass with crushed ice. Add the tequila and grenadine; slowly fill with orange juice. Stir gently.

TEQUILA MANHATTAN (SWEET)

6 to 8 ice cubes

2 splashes Angostura

¾ oz. sweet vermouth

1½ oz. tequila

Mix in a stirring glass. Strain into an iced cocktail glass with a maraschino cherry.

TEQUILA MANHATTAN (DRY)

Substitute dry vermouth for sweet vermouth.

TEQUILA MANHATTAN (MEDIUM)

Use a combination of dry and sweet vermouths.

TEQUINI

6 to 8 ice cubes

1 splash Angostura

2 to 3 splashes dry vermouth

1¾ oz. tequila

Mix in a stirring glass. Serve in an iced cocktail glass with a lemon twist or an olive.

TEQUILA SOUR

3 or 4 ice cubes

¾ oz. lemon or lime juice

1 to 2 teaspoons sugar

1¾ oz. tequila

Mix in a shaker. Serve in a whisky sour glass. Garnish with a maraschino cherry.

TEQUILA COLLINS

Mix the Tequila Sour in a highball glass. Stir well and fill with soda water. Garnish with a maraschino cherry.

TEQUILA & MESCAL

TEQUILA FIZZ

3 or 4 ice cubes

1 oz. lemon juice

½ oz. sugar syrup

1¾ oz. tequila

soda water

Mix all but the soda water in a shaker. Serve in a highball glass; top with the soda water. Garnish with a lemon slice or a maraschino cherry.

BRAVE BULL

6 to 8 ice cubes

1 oz. Tia Maria

1 oz. tequila

Stir the tequila and Tia Maria with the ice cubes in a stirring glass. Strain into a sherry glass and top with lightly whipped cream.

TEQUILA MARIA

3 or 4 ice cubes

¼ oz. lemon juice

3 oz. tomato juice

1¾ oz. tequila

black pepper, celery salt, Worcestershire sauce, Tabasco, to taste

Season to taste and mix in a shaker. Serve in a highball glass. (This can also be stirred with ice in a highball glass.)

CARABINIERI

1 scoop crushed ice

¼ oz. lemon juice

2¾ oz. orange juice

1 egg yolk

¾ oz. Galliano

1 oz. tequila

Mix in a blender with the crushed ice. Pour into a highball glass half filled with crushed ice.

MEXICANA

crushed ice

¾ oz. lemon or lime juice

1½ oz. pineapple juice

1 splash grenadine

1¾ oz. mescal

Mix in a shaker with 1 scoop crushed ice. Strain into a highball glass and serve over fresh crushed ice.

MONTEZUMA

1 scoop crushed ice

1 egg yolk

1 oz. Madeira

1½ oz. mescal

Mix with the crushed ice in a blender. Serve in an iced cocktail glass.

TEQUILA MOCKINGBIRD

1 scoop crushed ice

juice of ½ lime

¼ oz. green crème de menthe

1½ oz. tequila

ice water or soda water

Mix in a highball glass with the crushed ice. Fill with ice water or soda water; stir.

CHAPALA

3 or 4 ice cubes

¾ oz. lemon or lime juice

1½ oz. orange juice

a splash of grenadine

¼ oz. Cointreau

1½ oz. tequila

Mix in a shaker. Strain into a highball glass half filled with crushed ice.

YELLOW BOXER   *1981

crushed ice

¾ oz. lemon juice

¾ oz. Rose's Lime Juice

¾ oz. orange juice

¼ oz. Galliano

1¾ oz. tequila

Mix in a shaker with 1 scoop crushed ice. Strain into a highball glass half filled with fresh crushed ice.

LATIN LOVER   *1984

crushed ice

¼ oz. lemon juice

¾ oz. Rose's Lime Juice

2 oz. pineapple juice

¾ oz. cachaça

1½ oz. tequila

Mix in a shaker with 1 scoop crushed ice. Shake vigorously. Strain into a highball glass half filled with fresh crushed ice. Garnish with a pineapple slice and maraschino cherry.

MALCOLM LOWRY   *1984

1 scoop crushed ice

¾ oz. lemon or lime juice

¾ oz. Cointreau

¾ oz. white rum

1 oz. mescal

Mix in a shaker with the crushed ice. Serve in an iced cocktail glass with a salted rim.

PEPE   *1984

crushed ice

¼ oz. lemon or lime juice

1½ oz. grapefruit juice

a splash of Cointreau

¾ oz. cachaça

1 oz. tequila

Mix in a shaker with 1 scoop crushed ice. Strain into a highball glass half filled with fresh crushed ice.

Refreshing drinks made from tropical fruit juices and the Brazilian sugarcane brandy cachaça are known by the natives as *batidas*. The amount of cachaça in them is very small and it is common to see *batidas* mixed right in the glass with the ice. Cachaça, like many types of rum, is distilled directly from the sap of the sugarcane, after it has fermented for roughly three weeks in a copper or wooden vat, and then concentrated by repeated boiling. The best-known cachaça is Pitú, produced in Vitoria de Santo Antao, some twenty-five miles west of Recife. Other imported cachaças include Negâ Fulô from Brazil and Aguardiente Cristal from Colombia.

Cachaça became popular abroad mainly on account of the favorite drink of the Brazilians: the *Caipirinha* or "peasants' drink" (*caipira* = peasant). The original recipe for the Caipirinha calls for only cachaça, lime juice, and sugar.

CAIPIRINHA

1 lime

2 oz. cachaça

1 to 2 teaspoons sugar, to taste

1 scoop crushed ice

Quarter the lime and squeeze into a highball glass. Add the cachaça and sugar to taste. Stir, fill with ice, stir again. Garnish with another quarter of lime.

BATIDA BRASIL

1 scoop crushed ice

¾ oz. batida de coco

1 oz. cachaça

2¾ oz. coconut cream

Mix in a highball glass. Stir well.

CAIPIROSKA

Mix as for the Caipirinha, but substitute vodka for cachaça.

CAIPIRISSIMA

Mix as for the Caipirinha, but use white rum in place of cachaça.

BATIDA CARNEVAL

1 scoop crushed ice

1 oz. cachaça

1 oz. orange juice

2¾ oz. mango juice

Mix in a highball glass. Stir well.

Batida de Maracuja

1 scoop crushed ice

½ of a passion fruit, quartered,
or 2 oz. maracuja juice

1 splash lime juice

1 oz. cachaça

Mix in a blender. Serve in a highball glass over ice.

Batida de Coco

1 scoop crushed ice

¾ oz. batida de coco

¼ oz. cream

1½ oz. pineapple juice

1 oz. cachaça

Mix and serve as for the Batida de Maracuja.

Copacabana

1 scoop crushed ice

¾ oz. cream

2 oz. papaya juice

¾ oz. chocolate syrup

1¾ oz. cachaça

Mix and serve as for the Batida de Maracuja.

Batida de Banana

1 scoop crushed ice

1 banana

1½ oz. pineapple juice

¾ oz. cream

1 oz. cachaça

Mix and serve as for the Batida de Maracuja.

On the 14th, at daybreak, Captain Cook sent his launch and Captain Furneaux another boat, to the isle of O-Tahà, which was two or three leagues distant and enclosed in the same reef within which we lay at anchor. They were in hopes of purchasing some fruit there, which was very scarce at Raietea, and to that purpose provided Lieutenant Pickersgill and Mr. Rowe, the mate of the *Adventure*, with a quantity of beads and nails. Dr. Sparrman and my father were unwilling to miss this opportunity of examining another island and likewise embarked with them.

Having been invited to come and dine on the shore by Orèa, the chief of this part of the island, the captains with several officers and passengers of both ships and myself went on shore about noon, taking with us a little pepper and salt, some knives, and a few bottles of wine. A great part of the chief's spacious house was spread with quantities of leaves, which served as a tablecloth round which we seated ourselves with the principal inhabitants. We had not waited long before one of the common people arrived with a hog smoking on his shoulders, roasted whole, and wrapped in a large bundle of plantain leaves, which he threw upon the floor in the midst of us: a second tossed a smaller to us in the same manner; and these were followed by several others bringing baskets full of breadfruit, bananas, and the fermented paste of breadfruit, called *ma-hei*.* Our host now desired us to help ourselves and in a short time we had cut the two hogs in pieces. All the women and the common sort of people applied to us with a begging tone for portions, and what we distributed was handed from our neighbors to the remotest persons in the crowd. The men consumed their share with every mark of a good appetite, but the women carefully wrapped theirs up and preserved it till they should be alone. The eagerness with which they repeated their importunities, as well as the envious looks of the chiefs whenever we granted the request, convinced us that the commonality were in this island deprived of all sorts of luxuries and dainties.

We all agreed that the pork set before us tasted infinitely better than if it had been dressed after the European manner. It was much juicier than our boiled, and more tender beyond comparison than roasted meat. The equal degree of heat with which it stews underground had preserved and concentrated all its juices. The fat was not luscious and surfeiting, and the skin—instead of being hard as stone, which is always the case with our roasted pork—was as tender as any other part.

After dinner our bottles and glasses

were brought in, and our friend Orèa drank his share without flinching, which appeared to us rather extraordinary since almost all the natives of these islands expressed a great dislike to our strong liquors. Sobriety is a virtue almost universal with them, and particularly among people of inferior rank. They are, however, acquainted with an intoxicating beverage, which is much admired by some of the old chiefs. It is made in the most disgustful manner that can be imagined, from the juices contained in the root of a species of pepper tree. This root is cut small and the pieces chewed by several people, who spit the macerated mass into a bowl where some water (milk) of coconuts is poured upon it. Then they strain it through a quantity of the fibers of coconuts, squeezing the chips, till all their juices mix with the coconut milk; and the whole liquor is decanted into another bowl. They swallow this nauseous stuff as fast as possible, and some old topers value themselves on being able to empty a great number of bowls. I was present at the whole process one of the first days after our arrival at this island. Our passenger Porea, who was not so reserved with the natives here as he had been at Huahine, brought one of his new acquaintances into the captain's cabin and immediately sat down with him to perform the operation. He drank about a pint, which in less than a quarter of an hour made him so dead drunk that he lay down on the floor without motion; his face was inflamed and his eyes swelled out of his head. A sound sleep of several hours was necessary to restore him to his senses, but as soon as he had recovered them he appeared thoroughly ashamed of his debauch.

The pepper plant is in high esteem with all the natives of these islands as a sign of peace, perhaps because getting drunk together naturally implies good fellowship. It seems, however, that drunkenness here is punished, like all other excesses, by disease. The old men who make a practice of it are lean, covered with a scaly or scabby skin, have red eyes, and red blotches on all parts of the body. They acknowledge these evils to be the consequence of drinking; and to all appearance the pepper plant, which they call *awa*, tends to produce leprous complaints.

INDEX

Arranged alphabetically

INDEX

Arranged by chapter

Daiquiris. Reprinted with permission of Charles Scribner's Sons an imprint of Macmillan Publishing Company from *Islands in the Stream* by Ernest Hemingway. Copyright © 1970 Mary Hemingway. Published in Great Britain by Collins Publishers.

Cuba Libre. Copyright © Jules de Palm. From *Antiya* by Jules de Palm, published in 1981 by De Bezige Bij, Amsterdam. Translated by Klaske Piebenga.

The Magic Potion. Excerpts from *Wedding at Port-au-Prince* by Hans Christoph Buch, copyright © 1986 by Harcourt Brace Jovanovich, Inc., reprinted by permission of the publisher.

At Mère Catherine's. From THE COMEDIANS by Graham Greene. Copyright © 1965, 1966 by Graham Greene. All rights reserved. Reprinted by permission of Viking Penguin Inc.

Punch and Profit. Excerpt from TWO SERIOUS LADIES from THE COLLECTED WORKS OF JANE BOWLES. Copyright © 1943, 1966 by Jane Bowles. Reprinted by permission of Farrar, Straus and Giroux, Inc. Jane Bowles TWO SERIOUS LADIES published by Peter Owen, London.

The Rum Shop. Reprinted by permission of the Putnam Publishing Group and the author from PRAISESONG FOR THE WIDOW by Paule Marshall; © 1983 by Paule Marshall.

Miss Ida's Cafe. Excerpt from THE HARDER THEY COME by Michael Thelwell. Reprinted by permission of Grove Press, a division of Wheatland Corporation. Copyright © 1980 by Michael Thelwell.

Under the Volcano. Approximately six pages from UNDER THE VOLCANO by Malcolm Lowry. Copyright © 1947 by Malcolm Lowry. Reprinted by permission of Harper & Row, Publishers, Inc. and the Executors of the Malcolm Lowry Estate.

Oaxaca—Around the Farolito Today. Copyright © Libération. Reprinted from "Garçon, un bidon de mescal!" by Philippe Garnier, in *Libération*, June 26, 1986. Reprinted by permission of Libération. Translated by Richard Miller.

Set in Bodoni and Universe by Trufont
Typographers, Inc., New York, NY.
Printed by Toppan Printing Company
Ltd., Tokyo, Japan.